Rambling by RV
Through
Alaska & Yukon Territory

This is not your typical Alaska travel log! You will find between these covers: adventures to explore; stories to enjoy (some true); history to contemplate; things to do and places to go; tempting morsels to taste (yum); hints for planning your trip and fish to catch.

NYLA WALSH

Enjoy Rambling
Nyla Walsh

Printed by Gorham Printing, U.S.A.

ISBN 10: 0-9785788-1-3
ISBN 13: 978-0-9785788-1-7

CONTENTS

If you think you must read this book from front to back you will be mistaken! Please feel free to turn to which ever area of the book that most interests you and start reading.

DEDICATIONS & ACKNOWLEDGEMENTS

I dedicate this book to my friends and family and acknowledge all the love and support I received during this project:

First Suzanne Williamson for catching all (I'm sure) of my grammar and spelling boo boos and for giving me so many helpful ideas and gentle pushes along the way. I needed all the help I could get. Her husband, LeRoy for letting me keep her busy. Their friendship is treasured.

My family who made themselves scarce, when I wanted to throw things, like this #*!@?!*?# computer (without which, I could not have put this book together) and gave me suggestions, that I often ignored (at first anyway). They know I really do love them! To my loving husband, Lorrin, who traveled every mile of this Grand Adventure with me. Without him, I would still be planning the trip. I want to give a very special thanks to our youngest granddaughter Kirsty, who was the artist for some of the cute little creatures in this book. I hope you enjoy them as much as I do.

From my past, my Mom and Dad who told me I could do anything that I put my mind to. Writing a book is the last thing they would have thought I would do and yet it would not surprise them that I did.

And finally, I dedicate this book to all of you that have traveled up north and loved it the way we do; those of you yet to travel to the Great Land but are thinking about going and those that want an armchair adventure without the potholes and frost heaves. Enjoy being a part of our adventure if only vicariously. I would like to give you the desire to go for the first time or go again. **See you all on the Alcan!**

PREFACE

I have dreamed of going north since I was a teenager, long, long ago. Two of my uncles worked on the Alcan Highway during WW II. I grew up hearing bits and pieces of their stories.

Doris Tegstrom a friend of my mother's had driven the Alcan Highway first in 1948 and many times thereafter. She lived and worked in the Anchorage area for many years. Every so often she would come by for a visit and put dreams of the Last Frontier into my head. She even suggested that I come up for the summer after I graduated from high school to work and do some travel in 1965. My folks thought it would be a wonderful experience for me to spend a few months in the wilderness and then come back home to get my education. Right mother--- that's what I was going to do, sure it was! In my teenage mind, I figured if I ever got to go up there I would stay, not come back! Great North, here I come!! I wanted that Jack London experience! Yippy!

Well, the earthquake of 1964 took care of my plans for the great escape. Doris's home and business were both destroyed during that disastrous quake. No place for me to stay or to work after she moved to her family cabin on Kenai Lake, far from Anchorage. Her stories about living in that log cabin with no electricity or modern plumbing only strengthened my desire to head north. One story that stands out in my memory is the time Doris had taken her morning trek to the "little house," you know the one with the crescent moon on the door. When she opened the door to return to her cabin, the door unceremoniously hit a moose on its rump. Indignantly the moose took off running in one direction, as fast as Doris ran in the other direction!

Mother got her way, as she always did. Yes --- Mother! I studied to become a Licensed Practical Nurse as was the plan all along. Turns out that it was a good thing too! As I met my "husband to be" the summer of 65! Thoughts of Alaska and wild adventures were put on hold while we married and raised two fine boys.

I did get to Alaska finally in 1989 and I have gone back every year since! No, I didn't move to Alaska, drive or fly there either. I worked on cruise ships, sailing the waters of southeast Alaska each summer and sailing the world the rest of each year. Oh, the stories I could tell of those many years traveling the high seas! Well that is another book in itself and most of the stories that I could tell, you wouldn't believe anyway!

My next step into Alaska and Yukon Territory was as a Tour Director taking folks into the wilderness to see the beauty of this Great Land. The problem with that was once I experienced Alaska, I wanted more and until you do experience it, you have no idea how much "more" there is. I didn't get to stop and stay where I wanted. I dreamed of doing more, staying longer!

I will say that a trip on a lavish ship and in a luxury coach with a driver and a guide to tell the stories and point out the nuances, catering to your every need along the way, is a great way to go, especially if you have never been before.

The last three winters Lorrin and I have been on the road across America and Canada, with a big tour bus, promoting land and sea travels in Alaska and Yukon Territory.

I believe all the years I have spent working my way in and around Alaska has brought me to this point. I am ready to go into the wild and "not" get eaten by a griz! I hope!

The summer of 2008, at long last, we traveled for ourselves, in our own motorhome, stopping where we wanted and taking our time along the way.

When I started this book I was not sure of the story it would tell. Don't expect this to be your typical Alaska travel log. I will let it take me where it will and hope you will find it entertaining, helpful and interesting too.

So why am I writing this book? There are so many already written about Alaska!

Well, my husband told me I should and I always do what he tells me to do! Yes --- DEAR! The truth be known, I love sharing my knowledge and my love for adventuring in the land of the Midnight Sun, with folks like you.

Before we get started, I should introduce my husband, as he did come along on this Adventure! Lorrin is my husband; traveling partner; trip planner; mechanic and soul mate of 42 years. He retired after 38 years of civil service work, is now a driver for a tour bus company, has been a driving instructor and most recently, he has written and published a book *"How to Drive your Mortorhome like a Pro,"* as well as a **DVD** that he and Mark Polk (of RV Education 101) produced, that complements his book. *(It never hurts to advertize, right)*.

ITEMS TO NOTE

These symbols are scattered throughout the book for a little fun and to help you find information.

Tree = *did you know* = a factoid or some tidbit that will help you enjoy the Great North.

Beaver = *as the story goes* = there is most likely more than one version of the story told about the same event. I will tell you the one I think is true, or maybe the one I like the best, true or not! I may even tell you more than one version leaving it up to you to decide for yourself which is true, as one thing is certain in the Far North. There are as many versions of a story as there are people telling it. Facts and truths sometimes have little in common.

Moose = *hints or moose nuggets* = a helpful idea.

Inukshuk = *top picks or musts* = giving you direction to something that we think you should not miss.

Mountain = *debunk the myths* = what you have heard to be true, just might be a "myth". I would like you to know the real facts.

Eagle = **prose** = original works from my pen.

At the end of each adventure you will find animals noted, along with a number in [ ] followed by where we saw them, i.e. [3] [YT, AK]. The number notes how many of that particular animal we have seen. A short story about why I have highlighted that particular animal.

INTRODUCTION

Are you planning on going to Alaska and Yukon Territory? Have you traveled the Alcan yourself and remember when you last went? Or would you like to read about someone's wanderings and random thoughts about the Great North? If so, this book is for you!

So you want to drive to Alaska and all those places up north?!? "WHY" would one want to do that, it is "SOOOO" cold and snowy up there? Wrong, or at least not all the time! I will set you straight on that thought and some others that you think to be true about Alaska and Yukon Territory.

Think about it. You are going to travel long distances. Yep, Alaska is the "Biggest state". More than twice as big as Texas, one fifth the size of the lower 48! Mile after mile of, mile after mile! Many of their highways aren't even paved!

You will have to get use to all those hours of sun, in the land of the "Midnight Sun."

You will see few people along the way. Half of Alaska's population lives in and around Anchorage.

There are animals out there. No, not "herds" of Grizzly Bears roaming across the Serengeti, but if you take time along the way you will have some really "great" encounters with many of the animals of the north. Bears don't herd and it is the Tundra, not the Serengeti. The incredible scenery, mountains, valleys, rivers, vast reaches of tundra for as far as you can see and beyond! Where if you desire, you can toss a hook into a stream or lake and pull out dinner for four! How about a few gold nuggets and there are always salmon and halibut out in the ocean waiting to be caught.

Oh and the history from before written time, right up to present day!

The air up north is so fresh that you just have to breathe deeply! There is nothing like it!

Towns with names like Chicken, Tok, Mayo, Deadhorse, Clam Gulch, for every name, a story can be told. Then there are names that spell check and my tongue do not recognize, like, Ninilchik, Talkeetna, Kantishna and Schwatka.

Hey wait a minute! I think I get it!! These are really reasons "TO" go, not, "NOT" to go!!!

For the record, I have named our motorhome *"Rika" the Road House*. Why Rika, you may ask? Yes there is a story to go with the name, of course there is! Think about it, the motorhome is a traveling house, isn't it? So isn't it a road house, motorhome, road house, house on the road. OK, alright, it's corny, so live with it!! Those of you that have been to Alaska may recall, Rika's Road House at Big Delta State Historical Park. We are fond of this beautiful roadhouse on the Tanana River. More about this site later, when we once again stop for a slice of strawberry-rhubarb pie ala mode or maybe this time a bear-claw will tempt us. Yummmy!

Along that line of thought I have also named our little car that we tow behind Rika. Most folks call their tow cars Tow or Toad. Me, I have to be different! It is a Sidekick (Suzuki) which I shortened to the *Kick*. From this time forward if you see "the Kick" in the book it is our little, gas saving run about. If you see "Rika" it is our comfy motorhome.

I have chosen not to record daily events, instead, writing every few days, about the past few. Each chapter will be an "Adventure" as we have had many along the way. Bits of trivia, historical notes, facts and stories (some may be true) will enhance each adventure. You will enjoy reading this book as much as we have had experiencing our adventures!

If you are interested in recipes that I have whipped up while on this trip, you will find some of them in  "Adventures in Cooking on the Road".

If you are planning to go on your own adventure, just dreaming, or maybe you have been up north in the past and want to remember when ---!

It's time to turn the page and get started!

RVers on the road, ready to start their Alaskan adventure.

Rika at Mile "0" in Dawson Creek B.C. (Alcan Highway)

The Kick and Rika ready for a quite night of camping.

Rika under the pipeline, near the Yukon R. Crossing
Visitor Contact Station.

SHAKEDOWN ADVENTURE #0

Because of the type of work we have done for the last three years, I have not had the opportunity to do much driving. That means no time to get comfortable with our new motorhome. Before we started north we made a quick trip to the East Coast to film Lorrin's "new" DVD about how to drive your motorhome.

"Now"---I get to drive---I like driving---I really do!
OK, recap:
Long time, not driving
Husband has written a book about driving RV's!
He is the "Expert"
He is a driving instructor
New motorhome
Forced sprint across country and back before we head north.
Ladies, do you have shivers running up your spine yet?
No pressure here! Right!!

I figure this is a good thing. We'll take a shakedown trip. Make sure all the widgets and whatnots are onboard, the need not's aren't and all those new rig bugs are worked out. Make sure that I in fact can keep the motorhome on the road. Oh yes, that we can survive each other on such a long adventure.
The first leg from Silverdale, Washington to Fayetteville, North Carolina took 5 days and we traveled 2990 miles. There was an earthquake in Tennessee as we were passing through.
I think it was caused by the sonic boom that we created along the way. We encountered snow, high winds and rain and kept

the shinny side up. I only closed my eyes once, while I was crossing a bridge that was under construction, (10 foot lane) Oh joy! Lorrin's drive instruction really works! **Wow!**

Our motorhome preformed well and held together, as did we! I did some relief driving and Lorrin was a perfect gentleman (drive instructor). I am sure that he would have liked to point out some of my many driving short comes. He knows that I am trying and I don't think I did too badly or I am sure that he would have let me know!

The filming for the DVD went well and fast. You will especially like the bloopers. A star was born! (On sale now)

Now the return trip starts. This is why it is good to take a shakedown trip. We started to lose coolant and decided by the time we got to Denver that we should not go any farther. We made a few calls and ended up at a repair shop. In short order they found the problem, a broken radiator clamp. Thank the RV Guardian Angels, that it wasn't any worse. The clamp was replaced and we were under way in short order. We again experienced rain, snow, sleet, and wind on our return trip. The next problem to come along was the wind tried to remove the slide-out's awning from the side of our motorhome. At that point, we thought it prudent to pull off and wait for the wind to calm down. The awning is no worse for wear and we will now know that if it starts to flap again, it is time to get off the road and wait for the wind to abate. We traveled 3160 miles and took 7 days for our return trip.

Yes, we survived each other too! I did drive most everyday and we did not go for any choke holds! This truly was a good chance to check things out and make sure all was working, as well as giving me the chance to get some drive time in. I must admit that Lorrin did a bang up job of letting me get comfortable behind the wheel. I am grateful for that. Ladies, he is a keeper! *Now if he can just get that sock out of his mouth, everything will be fine!*

Here are a few questions that I have been asked while I worked onboard cruise ships in Alaska:

Where does the ship get its power?
> *(A really long extension cord)*

Is this cable or satellite television?
> *(You guess)*

What time will we see the whales?
> *(I didn't know they were under contract as yet)*

Does this elevator go to the front of the ship?
> *(Say what?)*

Is the water in the toilet salt water or fresh water?
> *(I don't even want to know why they asked!)*

Will it rain while I am in Alaska?
> **(<u>YES!</u>)**

I could write a whole book on the questions I have been asked!

The land up there is really -- really BIG!

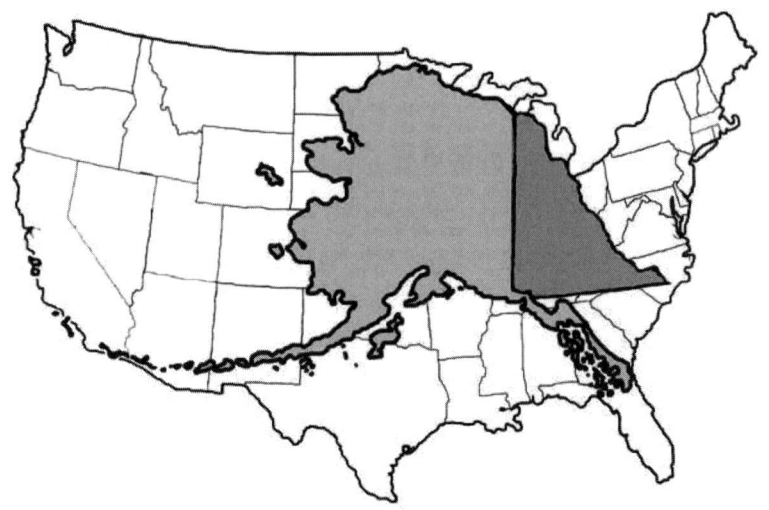

Alaska is one fifth the size of all the 48 continental states put together – has 33,000 miles of coast line – has more than ½ the world's glaciers - has the tallest mountain in North America, McKinley at 20,320' and for you Texans, Alaska is 2.3 times the size of the state of Texas

ADVENTURE #1

(For reference we started out April 19th 2008)
*Day 1-3 = Home, Silverdale, WA * Sumas, border crossing into*
*Canada * Chilliwack, BC - camped * Lac La Hache, BC - camped **
Solitude Mountain Lodge, near Chetwynd, BC – camped

The day is really here! Time to go! Are we ready? Of course
we are! With guide books and maps in hand and cupboards full,
we are off. One can over plan and prepare for a trip like this.
No matter how much we prepare there will be something that
we did not think to do or to bring. No worries; there are stores
along the way in which we can get what we need.

Our first day takes us as far as Chilliwack, BC. In keeping with
the plan of slowing down, we drove back roads (hwy 9) skirting
the foothills of the Cascades instead of Interstate 5 north. We
are trying to pace ourselves as we often tend to go too far and
to fast each day when we are traveling. We remind ourselves
that we should stop and smell the roses along the way.
Reminder to self, each day of this adventure, "**is the
destination**," "and we intend to enjoy every day's adventure!"
We are very lucky as we have as much time as we want and we
are going to use it to its fullest!

Next we travel to Lac La Hache, BC and on to Chetwynd, BC.
Ok if you are following on a map you will notice, we have
zoomed a bit more then planed.   We have found that one
of the things we like to remind others of, "early in the season
not everything is open." This statement caught up with us along

about now.   Even though the guide books said that the campsites would be open by this time, many were not yet open. It is spring time, don't you know.   We find that the camp grounds both government and private tend to get started with the season.   If spring is late, so will their opening time.   It takes time to shake off winter, push back the snow and mend the water pipes before opening up for business.

It never ceases to amaze me, as we travel the highways and byways of North America, the wonders we see!    It is hard to remember that the distances are great, yes even farther than one can imagine!   You can look at a map all you want, but until you take the drive, it does not hit you that it is the GREAT (BIG) NORTH COUNTRY, for sure!

As we started north this spring I really enjoyed the budding flowers and greening trees along the way.   It brought to mind something I wrote along while ago.   Thought you might like to read it.

FLOWERS IN SPRING

The beauty of spring was outside my door,
As I hurried by with no time at all.
At first I didn't even see
Winter had slipped away.
Then by chance
(Or was it?)
I happened to glance that way.
Oh! What beauty there was to behold.
So tiny, so delicate its petals of white said to me
"Take time my friend"
"Take time to see."
"All around you is Nature's beauty!"

2

It caught me by surprise
Like a rainbow after a shower.
I took time, and now say to you
Beauty is near by
If "YOU" will just take the time,
My friend!

Often visitors traveling to Alaska forget that British Columbia and Yukon Territory are part of the trip, zipping straight through without a second glance. We have driven through this country many times and even though our plan is to slow down, we have opted to save the first few days for future, shorter trips, from home. It is not enough to say, "This area is rich in beauty, history, nature and heritage." It deserves time of its own for exploring in depth. As this trip is about the Greatland, Alaska and Yukon, this will be my focus, in this book.

Elk *[3]* & **Mule Deer** *[23], [BC, YT] one of our special memories this summer was the brand new wobbly legged Elk calf that was standing next to the road. We were lucky to see both Elk and Mule Deer on our trip as there are few of either that live in the far north.*

Why did the moose cross the road? To show his best side for the tourist's camera!

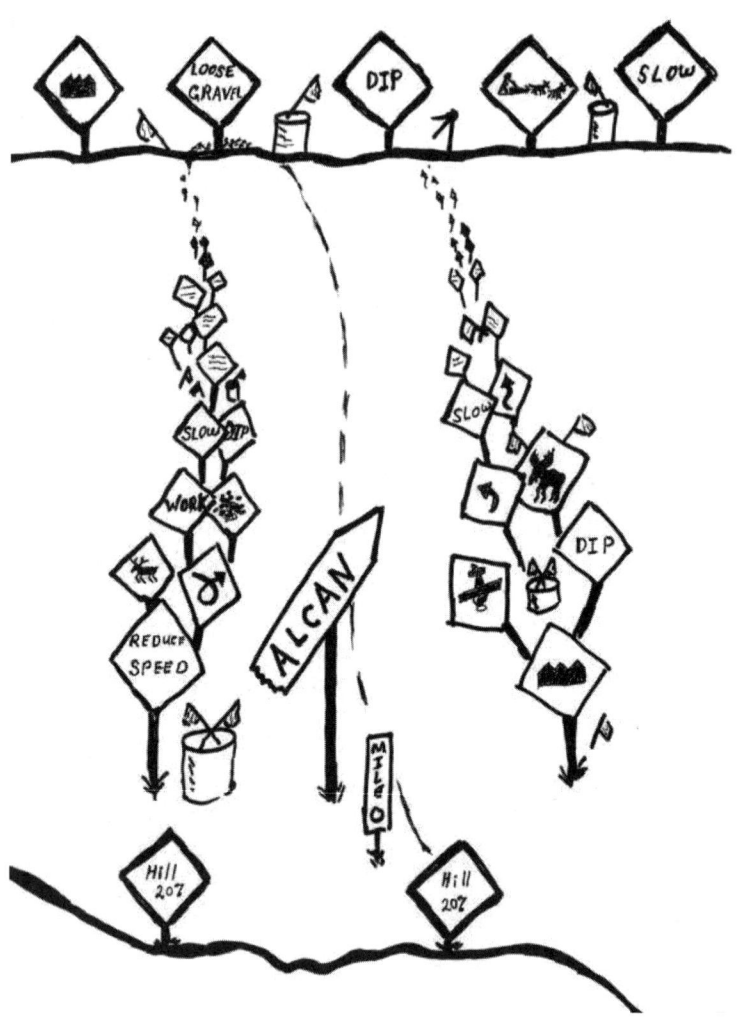

Is this what you think the Alcan Highway looks like?

ADVENTURE #2

Day 4-7 = Dawson Creek, BC (mile "0" of the Alcan Hwy) camped
* Pink Mountain, BC - camped * Fort Nelson, BC – camped

Dawson Creek, BC mile post "0" is the official beginning of the Alcan Highway. Even though we have been on the road for six days, this is the real start of the trip for us! I have traveled the northern portion of the Alcan many times in past years; this will be the first time for me on the southern portion of the Alcan.

We spent a few days in Dawson Creek BC exploring this town named for George Mercer Dawson, a surveyor. The work he did in 1879 encouraged farmers to settle in this area. The Canadian Pacific Railway soon arrived, helping to further expand Dawson Creek. When the construction of the Alcan Highway began, this railroad was instrumental in getting the supplies to the troops and civilian engineers building the highway.

There are many beautiful murals depicting its rich history to view as you walk throughout this historic town. Each year they add a few new murals to honor the hard working men and women from the town's past.

Lorrin bought a gold pan in town, with visions of striking it rich! Oh goody, we will soon be rolling in gold!

Even thou it was overcast and drizzly the morning we set out on the Alcan Highway, we did not let it detour us from enjoying the day and remind ourselves that it is still early in the year. Because it seemed the right thing to do, we drove back into town, to the official start of the highway, at 102nd Ave and 10th St. We had to take the "traditional" photo with Rika parked in front of the mile post, marking Mile "0", the official start of the Alcan Highway in Dawson Creek. You may ask, "What is a mile post anyway? For those of you that don't know, the story goes like this. While the road was under construction the builders used the number of miles from Dawson Creek as a way of describing where they were working along the route. When the Alcan was opened to the public after WW II, communities and services were established along the route. Mile posts were maintained to help those traveling the highway. In this manor they could tell how far it was to the next stop or how far they had come along the highway. Soon folks along the way used the mile post numbers as their address and they are still used in this way today. However, this has become somewhat convoluted as the road has been re-engineered over the years, curves have been straightened and by-passes have been made. The original posts are no longer there or accurate and oh yes and to add to the confusion, in Canada it is now kilometers instead of miles! I remind myself this just adds to the fun of traveling the highway. Was that a historic mile post that just went by? Or was that a current mile post and was that kilometers or miles? Maybe it helped the travelers of old, but I am not so sure about "this" traveler, today! It added to the challenge when Lorrin asked me, "how far is it to the next turnout?" OMG! Get over it, sit back and enjoy the scenery, we will be there sooner or later, I think. We aren't in any rush, are we? Was that an overreaction on my part, well maybe, just a little? OK, so I apologized! Does that work for you?

We have made comments to each other as we travel the Alcan, that many of the freeways and toll ways we have traveled on in the lower 48 aren't nearly as smooth as the Alcan is today. Believe me, we should know what a rough road is, having worked the last three winters crisscrossing the highways and byways of the U.S. and Canada.

As we drive along the newer sections of the highway, we can catch glimpses of the old highway winding back and forth. Boy, are we thankful for the smooth, wide road we are now on. My thoughts are often drawn back to what it must have been like when they where building the road and what must have been the thoughts of those folks working in such adverse conditions that they could not even imagine before they arrived into this vast wilderness. Would we, today, have the strength and endurance to prevail? The civilians who first traveled this route must have been made of true grit as well!

A short way down the highway, we make a turn off the new road onto the old road for a short side trip. Now we are even happier that they have improved the highway! Can you spell bumpy, curvy and narrow? This was a must do detour, as it took us over the Alcan's last remaining original curved, wooden bridge, still in use today. The Kiskatinaw River Bridge is 534 feet long, 100 feet tall and has a 9 degree curve in its span. No wonder they sometimes call the building of this road one of the modern wonders of the world! I always think, when hearing a description such as this, how will the next bridge along the way be described, so it can be important too? Will it be taller, longer or older?

The rest of the day was spent enjoying the views and marveling at just how little there is to distract us from the natural beauty of this land. Civilization is stretched thin with lots of elbowroom for all who live here.

The Alcan (acronym for Alaska-Canada Highway) was built during World War II to connect Alaska with the lower 48 states. After the invasion of Pearl Harbor, the U.S. felt the need to better protect our countries west coast. President Roosevelt authorized the project, February 11, 1942, a formal agreement was soon secured to build a right-of-way between U.S. and Canada and construction got underway, March 9th, 1942. It took, 8 months and 12 days to complete this amazing project. There are books and documentaries (PBS has a good program on the building of the highway) about the adventures and hard times of the soldiers and civilians who worked together to blaze a road through muskeg and over mountains, crossing some of the most unforgiving land ever traversed, fighting off mosquitoes in the summer and subzero cold in the winter. I suggest that you pick up one or two books on the subject and get a better idea of the difficulties that were encountered along the route. Remember the original route was slashed through by the U.S. Army Corps of Engineers and at best was a "trail" that could accommodate vehicles, some of the time. The civilian contractors then set about making it more durable, all-season road, building bridges and otherwise making it more drivable. Work on the highway continues today, making it better in every way, for all us road warriors on the Alcan.

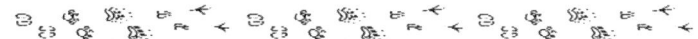

Dall's Sheep (Dall) [54ish] & ***Stone Sheep*** [11], [BC, YT] *Dall Sheep, otherwise known as the little white dots on the mountain, are on the cliffs if you know where to look and have a good spotting scope. We were lucky to see some up close. The best viewing, for us was in Denali NP. As for the Stone Sheep, they were standing on the road. We had to drive around them!*

A cartoon from my uncle's scrapbook. Uncle Charles must have had a lead foot on the Alcan!

Stone Sheep up close and personal!

Stone Sheep on the Alaska Hwy. (Alcan) in Northern BC. They were crossing the road at the proper crossing, well almost as that is a "Caribou" on the sign! They must have missed their crossing.

A family of Mallards enjoy Liard River Hotsprings Provincial Park.

ADVENTURE #3

Day 8-9 = Liard River Hotsprings, BC – camped

This day defines what my dreams are made of. We are underway early and our hopes are high for seeing some wildlife, as is promised by the guide books. The sun is already shining brightly, "the land of the midnight sun" comes to mind as we start to enjoy the long sunlit days of the north.

Moose, Bear, Caribou – even a Reindeer will do!
We've come to see you.
Please be kind and show us your antlers and paws too.
Will you grace us with your presence?
Or will you be shy hiding from our view?

This was a must do day and proved to be spectacular on all counts. We are in the Rocky Mountains, glass smooth waters of turquoise lakes reflecting snow covered peaks, rivers winding their way through valleys and yes, our hopes of wildlife came true, in great abundance. Mule Deer, Elk, Caribou, Stone Sheep, Bison, Coyote and Black Bear were enjoying the first rays of spring with us, not to mention birds of all description and little furry critters too. We stopped often to enjoy the serenity of this land, to listen to the sounds of nature and to breathe in air ever so fresh. It was a pleasure to slow down and take it all in. A special treat for us this day was the very new shaky legged elk calf standing alongside the road, mom watching from the tree

11

line a short distance away. My awe was tempered with the concern that the calf was too close to the road. I wanted to move the precious creature a little farther from the traffic and harm's way. Knowing that all the rules tell you not to approach wildlife, along with the thought of mom's very sharp hooves kept me in line and in the rig, as I should!

In the afternoon we pulled into Liard Hotsprings Provincial Park. 🌲One of the must do stops along the highway for an overnight stay and a relaxing dip in the hot springs. Ahhhh! The hot springs are comprised of two pools. A boardwalk winds its way into the woods through wetlands, first to Alpha pool and then a little farther to Beta pool. They fill naturally with water heated deep underground, reaching as much as 126 degrees F. Knowing that this area is known for its bears, I ask for reassurance from the rangers. They assured me that the bears that frequent the park are not in-residence as yet this spring. They said something about the bears liking to eat the dandelions and will show up when they are in bloom. I wonder if they are trying to put me at ease, no matter, I will keep a watchful eye on the bushes along the path, anyway! We are also told to watch out for Bison! 🐾 Did you know that more people in the world are killed and injured by hoofed animals than clawed animals? It's true!

This is where I must let you in on a little story about myself. All my life I have had a greater then reasonable fear of bears. Now it is good to have a healthy respect for them, but I am talking about a heart pounding, cold-sweat, don't want to get out of the rig, ever, kind of fear! This is, I have concluded, thanks to my two older brothers! Growing up in the Northwest, my family did a lot of tent camping. Places like Mt. Rainier and the Olympic

Mountains. In those days there were a lot (as I remember it) of bears and my loving, caring older brothers were more than helpful in pointing that fact out as often as possible. It went something like this "Nyla there's a bear behind you!" I would then give them the proper response, "EEEEEEEK" and run screaming to the nearest safe place, much to their delight! Sometimes there really was a bear there! This did not always go in their favor, as once I had locked myself in the car while my oldest brother tried to get some pictures of a bear. He had placed some crackers on a stump (I know, we don't do that anymore) and clicked away with his trusty, old camera. When the bear finished his snack, he took a look at my brother and thought, hmmm, maybe he has some more of those tasty crackers. No way would I open the locked, car door for him! Lucky for my brother the bear was not too hungry and soon wandered off. I seem to have more bear stories than most folks do. I think that the bears know I am frightened and want to help out, keeping up where my brothers left off! If I tried to tell all the stories, it would fill a book of its own, maybe there will be room for more stories later on. I just want you to understand, I no longer lock myself in the rig and I do take walks in the woods. Sometimes though I have to rally up my nerve to get out there and enjoy the wonder of nature (Lorrin knows to keep the bears at a safe distance, please and thank you very much!)

Liard Hotsprings, what a peaceful stop over! Even if you don't take a dip in the hot springs, the area is just too beautiful to miss! No bears in camp, yes! However we did see some bison walk by on the road. We didn't run after them, not wanting to add to the statistics of death by hoofs verses claws. The next day we could not bring ourselves to travel on, electing to stay one more night. We had another soak in the hot springs and a peaceful stroll on the boardwalk. The vegetation is amazing with many species unique to this area including of all things, orchids. The hot springs are an oasis-like microclimate. During the construction of the Alcan workers setup camp here and used the hot springs daily. Must have been nice!

In honor of all the "Sourdoughs" out there, I started my sourdough starter pot today. I want to see if it will work well while we travel. It will be fun to have flapjacks and such from sourdough started while we are on the road. One thing has just dawned on me, I did not bring even one recipe book. As a rule I don't do much fancy cooking while traveling. I think I might have to pick up a book on sourdough, as I have not worked with this yeasty concoction for a long time.

I am sure that you all have heard of sourdough and when you hear the term, think of the prospectors of California, Yukon and Alaska. 🌲 Did you know that it goes back in history as far as 4000 years, to Egyptian times and maybe even earlier? The miners treasured their sourdough starter as much as the gold they sought. They tended to it carefully, even to tucking it into their shirts next to their body to keep it warm and healthy during the cold winters. 🌲 Did you know that is why they were called "Sourdoughs?" They started to smell just like their starter. If you have ever smelled sourdough, you will understand. As long as they had the starter and some flour they could survive. It is said that wars were fought over prized starters. Some treasured starters were passed on from generation to generation. The famed San Francisco Sourdough Bread is said to be from a starter originating in the Gold Rush days of early California. Sourdough starters each have their own distinct taste and smell. Natural yeast organisms from the

14

air act together chemically, with the dough to give it the leavening action that makes the bread rise. I am interested in watching mine, to see if it will change flavor and action as we travel. It will be collecting different yeasts along the way. "Time will tell" as my momma would say.

Bison, [11], [BC] we saw these big guys on and next to the highway near Liard Hotsprings. Did you know that Bison were introduced into Alaska in the 1950s to restore the population lost 500 years ago? There are small, free ranging herds in Alaska, Yukon Territory and British Columbia.

Why is it? The relationship between the number of wildlife sightings and the number of safe pullouts never seem to match. See a moose and there won't be a pullout. See a pullout and there are no animals in sight. It must be a law or something!

Animals are the icing on the cake of this Great Land! Cherish each encounter!

Continental Divide

We crossed the Great Divide several times during our trip as it winds its way through Canada and Alaska.

ADVENTURE #4

*Day 10-13 = Swift River, YK (on the continental divide) camped ** *Whitehorse, YK - camped ** Side trips to - Carcross, YK - Fraser, BC - Skagway, AK*

We made stops in Watson Lake for the Signpost Forest snapshots and at the Northern Lights Centre. Both are worth the stop along the way. The Signpost Forest is unique to say the least! It was started in 1942, when Carl Lindley of Danville, IL put up the first sign, to remind him of how far he was from home. He was an U.S. Army soldier in Company D, 341st Engineers working the Alcan Highway. Today there are more than 60,000 signs in the collection as travelers have over the years added to the collection. We hope to have a sign for the forest when we come back through here in August. The Northern Lights Centre is dedicated to education of Aurora Borealis otherwise known as Northern Lights. A fascinating phenomena produced by charged electrons and protons reacting to gas particles in the earth's upper atmosphere.

I like to add that they can happen at any time, day or night, 365 days a year but we will not have a chance of seeing them until winter, as the sun stays up much too long in the summer. They are not visible unless it gets dark and what is going on this time of year? Yep, the sun is shining - you remember the land of the midnight sun and all. The three most important things that you need to see northern lights are: darkness, clear sky and solar flares. Oh yes, you have to be awake as well!

We stayed at a campsite situated on the Continental Divide near Swift River, YT. 🌲 If you think that the divide is a straight line, look at a map and see how the divide winds its way along cutting North America in half. At this point it divides two of the world's largest drainage systems; the Yukon River and the Mackenzie River watersheds. Water going west from this point flows into the Yukon and on to the Bering Sea and the Pacific Ocean and water going east joining together until it becomes the Mackenzie River and empties into the Beaufort Sea and Arctic Ocean. I have crossed the divide many places in North America and not really thought much about what it really was. So I looked up the definition to set myself straight. The Continental Divide or Great Divide is a mountain ridge which separates the watersheds that drain into the Pacific Ocean and those waters that flow into the Atlantic Ocean. Now I will note that there is a whole lot more to this explanation but this is the bottom line, simply stated.

The past few days have been a mix of travel and sightseeing. To me "travel" is the part where you are moving on down the road and making stops to see an overlook, go for a hike or just sit for awhile taking in everything around you. "Sightseeing" is the part where you are in a town, walking along the streets, checking out the shops and museums along the way. I am not the, got to see every store and museum type of person, though there are times that one must do that as well.

We set up camp in Whitehorse, YT for a few days, taking a side trip to Skagway with the Kick one day and wandering the streets of Whitehorse several days. This area has so many stories to tell, we had to take some extra time to enjoy.

This must do drive to Skagway is along the southern portion of the Klondike Highway and takes us not only through beautiful landscape but history as well. Along the way we added two more animal types to our list, a porcupine and mountain goats. We watched the goats frolic on the cliffs near the road. They were close enough for us to see very well. There were several kids in the group. Great pictures for the album! I love this drive, having taken it many times over the years as a tour director I can anticipate what is around each curve. We made stops at places like Emerald Lake, the name says it all! Carcross Desert, yes a desert right here along the highway - sand dunes and all. It is self proclaimed to be the smallest desert in the world. It was formed when a glacial lake left behind sand as it retreated. There are many unique varieties of vegetation here. The little town of Carcross was at one time a stop for the White Pass and Yukon Rail Road on its way to Whitehorse. It is situated on the banks of Lake Bennett, where the gold seekers sat waiting for spring breakup and built boats to float their supplies and themselves down river, to the gold fields. You must take a walk through town, buy an ice cream cone to munch and don't forget to check out the calaboose (jail) in The Barracks gift shop. The town used to be called Caribou Crossing but it was shortened to Carcross, as their mail was often sent to any number of other towns with the same name. The WP&YR, is no longer open to Whitehorse but still runs from Skagway to Carcross. It is a reasonably priced must do for those of you that would like to experience a narrow gauge rail that not only takes you on a scenic trip, it is your time machine back into the area's history and is fun to boot. You can get the current information on line or at the RR station in Skagway. There are many overlooks along the drive maybe too numerous to stop at everyone of them, but you must at least stop to watch the White Pass & Yukon Train as it takes passengers for a ride. Look for the gold trail that parallels the rail, carved into the side-hill by the gold-rushers heading into the goldfields, watch the wildlife and gaze at the mountains, valleys, lakes, waterfalls and streams.

At the end of the South Klondike Highway you come to the town of Skagway, nestled on the shores of Taiya Inlet. Skagway got its raucous beginning in 1897, with the Klondike Gold Rush. It popped up like a mushroom, over night, as thousands of the gold-seekers passed through Skagway on their way up either the White Pass Trail or Chilkoot Trail, to make their fortune in the goldfields of Dawson City and beyond. The legendary photograph taken of the gold seekers climbing the Golden Stairs of the Chilkoot Trail, with heavy packs on their backs, tells, without words, of the toil they endured and the tenacity they had, on their journey to fulfill their dream of riches awaiting them. They were required to take supplies weighing about 1200 lbs. (521 kilo) with them. The list of goods was prescribed and checked by the North-West Mounted Police. The supplies were supposed to be enough for the miners to survive a year in the gold fields. This was a very practical plan, on the Mounties part, as towns had not yet been built to supply the miners. The Mounties did not what to have a lot of folks starving and freezing to death on their watch. The miners climbed over snow covered mountains going to and fro, as many as 36 round trips for each miner, until all their goods were at the top of the pass. They built boats to transit Lake Bennett. They had to fight off thieves that wanted to steel their supplies and they crossed unforgiving terrain, in the worst of weather, just to get to Dawson City. It was an arduous adventure, full of danger. After their arrival in the goldfields, they still had to stake a claim, build a cabin, fight off claim jumpers not to mention dig, sluice and pan for the gold, oh yes and survive it all. To their disappointment, most of the claims were already staked by the pioneers and trappers already in the area before they arrived. Remember news traveled slowly in the 1800s. There was no instant messaging for them, in fact telegraph lines had not yet been strung. It took most of a year for news of the gold strike to reach the rest of the world and for the rushers to head north to the goldfields. By 1899 the stampede had all but ended. Skagway lived on after the stampede as the means into the interior via the soon to be completed, White Pass & Yukon Rail, connecting Skagway and Whitehorse. The legends of people like Soapy Smith (con artist), Frank Reid (good guy) and Klondike Kate (you guess) still come alive on the streets of Skagway today.

Be sure to check out the museums and shows for the history related to this historic town and places nearby like Dyea, a stampede town, that is now only a memory reclaimed by the wilderness, a few trails still wander through where the boom town once stood. Check with the park rangers at the Visitors Center for information about trail conditions and ratings before you go on any of these trails. If you want to get away from the hustle and bustle of the tourists in town, take a few steps away from Broadway St. and you are in the wilderness. If you are up to it you could hike the Chilkoot Trial (rated strenuous). This is the same trail the miners took to Lake Bennett. You can make arrangements with local services to take you to the beginning of the trail and pick you up 3-5 days later at the other end of the trail. Think about the miners as you climb. You will make this climb once and they climbed up with heavy packs about 36 times to transport all their supplies to the top and that was only the beginning of the journey for them. You on the other hand will get a comfortable ride back down the mountain, hot shower, hearty dinner and a soft bed when you get back to town. Skagway was originally spelled Skagua, this was a Tlingit word that meant "windy place." Today travelers of another kind have again swelled the town's population: tourists. They come in cruise ships, ferries, cars, RVs and on bikes. As in the past, those of us that visit Skagway today, leave some money behind, to the storekeepers delight. We like to say that the storekeepers of the past mined the miners as they often made more money selling goods to them, than the gold-seekers made in the fields. I think the same holds true today. I like the local artists and shops the best! Here is a hint. If you are looking to buy something made in Alaska or Yukon Territory or Native made while on your travels, look for a label to authenticate it is from AK and YT. (see the Glossary for what the labels look like) I like finding something special to remind me of our trip. I stopped by my favorite bookstore and picked up my Alaska sourdough cookbook, **Simply Sourdough -- The Alaska Way, By Kathy Doogan**. The starter is beginning to smell good and sour and it is showing signs of bubbling. I have made a few simple recipes such as pancakes and biscuits so far but I really want to try making bread to supplement our grocery needs.

White Pass and Yukon Rail was built during 1898 to 1900 because gold was found in the Klondike. The rail made it a little easier to get to the goldfields. It also was of great service during WW II getting supplies and workers to Whitehorse working on the Alcan Highway. Two of my uncles worked the project in 1942: Uncle Al (Allison) and Uncle Charles (Strum). I am sorry to say, I did not listen well enough to the stories they told, of their time working on the highway. When talking with my cousin Ernie, a short time ago, he showed me a scrapbook that his father had put together. I almost cried while I leafed through the pages, what a treasure he had in black and white photos, short notes, hand drawn cartoons, letters and mementoes. Uncle Charles had worked west of Whitehorse as a general superintendent for Dowell Construction, out of the W2 camp some 45 miles west of Whitehorse and by looks of it there were some good times to go along with the hard times! I, being one of the younger the cousins, thought I remembered that our grandfather Bates had worked on the highway too, but my older cousins say no. Strange though, when looking at a pamphlet about the highway I found reference to a Bates & Rogers Camp near to where my uncles had worked in the Yukon. From what I have found in the Yukon Archives in Whitehorse, there is no record of him being there. I will keep looking for information along the way.

Our day in Whitehorse, the capital of the Yukon, was spent again learning about the past and enjoying the present. ᚕHere museums and stores are all must do stops! You can learn about the Ice Age, Woolly Mammoths and the like, at the Beringia Interpretive Centre. Board the landlocked SS Klondike to hear the stories about sternwheelers on the Yukon and don't forget to make a stop at MacBride's Museum for more information of the area. Don't miss the walking tour that takes you by the skyscraper log cabin.

23

We also made a stop on the edge of town at Miles Canyon to walk across the suspension foot bridge. While I was busy taking pictures from the bridge a fox surprised us. I was standing in the middle of the bridge, Lorrin at the near end when a red fox wandered up on the far end. To our amazement it trotted a short ways onto the bridge and stopped as if waiting its turn to cross. When I did not move, it wandered back off the bridge and stepped to the side as if to say OK go ahead you cross first then. When I still did not move, it came back onto the bridge coming even closer to where I was standing. Having taken enough pictures I decided to start back. The fox followed me stopping to wait every time I looked over my shoulder. When I got off the bridge it passed us and wandered on along as if this was an everyday event for it.

The last few times we have stopped to camp, Lorrin has diligently washed Rika and the Kick, only to get back on the road and find a stretch of construction to coat the vehicles with dirt once again. I ponder the need of, to wash or not to wash, maybe we should not even try but then would the mud and dust weigh us down?

Mountain Goat [11], [AK] I always look for Mountain Goats on the hillsides as we travel to and from Skagway. Sometimes they can be quite close to the road. We spotted a few sheltered among the rocks, for protection from the, cool wet day. One cute little kid had found a cave and was standing at the entrance, dry and content while mom stood nearby in the rain.

Uncle Charles with a 25 # Lake Trout

Uncle Al at Soldiers Summit, YT

Our friendly Red Fox on the Miles Canyon suspension foot bridge near Whitehorse, YT.

Mountain Goat nanny and kid, southern Klondike Hwy.

ADVENTURE #5

*Day 14-20 = Kluane Lake, YT - camped * Border crossing, Beaver Creek, YK * Port Alcan, AK - camped * Tok, AK - camped * Slana, AK on the Nabesna Road - camped * Rufus Creek, AK on the Nabesna Road, Wrangell–St. Elias NP – camped*

We left Whitehorse feeling that even if we stayed a month we could not see it all! Just outside of town we took a side trip on an old section of the Alcan. This area was mentioned in my uncle's scrap book. We saw no evidence of a camp or logging mill along this stretch of gravel road that might have given us a clue as to where the camp may have been. We travel to Haines Junction and beyond, along the shores of Kluane Lake, where there was still ice piled up on the shores. It is very windy and we can see large dust clouds farther down the lakeshore, what a contrast! We have seen tour buses more often now and have made some stops at the same places, at the same time. It is fun to watch the passengers as they explore and discover the Great North. It brings back memories of the times I guided trips along these same highways on these same buses. I am so happy that this year is for us to enjoy in our own motorhome, just the two of us. We made must do stops at Kluane NP Visitor Centre, in Haines Junction for an overview, Kluane Museum in Burwash Landing, a great price for an even better natural history stop and Sheep Mountain Visitors Centre where we spotted a few Dall sheep on the mountain. We camped on the shores of Kluane Lake, at a beautiful, peaceful camp with a fabulous panorama of the lake. We are told to watch out for bears in the area. No worries, you know that I will keep my eyes open. You can count on that!

The next day we crossed the border at Beaver Creek, YT camping just across the border in Alaska. Along about now in our trip we are starting to enjoy, I say dubiously, the terms, frost heaves; dips; road work; pot holes; broken road; gravel on road and a myriad of other terms associated with this highway. We slow down as is recommended and travel on. The Alcan is starting to live up to its reputation, still it is far better than the stories we have heard about the terrors of travel along the highway north. We will not complain. As we drive into Tok, through old forest fire burns, I was reminded that wildfires happen in Alaska as often as they do anywhere else. You may not think that would be possible. This is often a misconception that we may have, "it can't burn up here it is too cold and wet, isn't it?" Wrong! There are many wildfires and they can get very big very fast. A fire near Tok, in July of 1990 burned more than 100,000 acres. The town was saved from burning to the ground, only when, what they refer to as a "miracle wind" turned the fire away from certain disaster.

Did you know Wildfires are a part of the life cycle of any forest, often starting from lightening strikes? Only when inhabited areas are threatened, such as in the Tok fire, will they fight a fire. Without fire once in a while, a forest will grow old and suffocate. A fire once in awhile helps the life cycle of a forest to continue. One tree for instance, the Black Spruce will only reproduce after fire releases its seeds from the cones. Fire also clears the underbrush so the tree's roots will not be smothered, adds nutrients to the soil, and controls disease and insect infestation. Our stop in Tok was pleasant respite from the bumps and frost heaves.

So what is a Tok? It is a town at the crossroads of the Alcan Highway and Tok Cutoff. It is the self proclaimed Dogsled Capital of the world. Now you may wonder how it got its name. The story goes and there are several versions (1.) Tok got its name when a surveyor was mapping out the area where two roads were to cross. He put an OK next to the X for the intersection of the two roads. Later someone thought that the X mark was a T and that the name of the area was Tok, hence the name Tok. (2.) The men building this section of the Alcan had a camp mascot, a dog, named Tok and decided to name the area for the dog. There are several other stories, one about Tokyo and one about a native word that sounded like Tok. You decide which is true or make up your own version, if you like. While at the RV camp in Tok a local singer and song writer, Dave Stancliff, entertained us with his music. We loved the songs so much that we bought all 3 of his CDs.

We leave the Alcan Highway at Tok and head south on the Tok Cutoff, to where we were told there maybe some Grayling waiting for us to catch. I gave myself a pep talk, "don't worry about the bears," grabbed my fishing gear and hiked ½ mile through the forest to a river. Sure enough we could see fish rolling and on my first cast I got a nice one. We spent about an hour catching and releasing the fish, keeping only a few for dinner.

Fishing in Alaska is one of the great pass times that most folks feel obliged to take part in during their travels up north. Most folks think only in terms of Salmon and Halibut when fishing in Alaska and the bigger the better! What we want to do most while we are here is, stream fishing. We don't have the chance to do much back home. Oh sure, we will hopefully get a guided salmon trip or two on the Kenai River, as one must, but for us it is not how many we catch, it is the fun of being outdoors, enjoying the surroundings and having a good meal of fresh caught fish, now and again. Isn't that what we are supposed to say? I am not an expert fisher person, so I have no great advise for you as to how to or where to fish. If you plan to do any fishing, I might suggest that you use barbless hooks even if it is not required, as you can release the fish you don't want to keep, with less harm to them. Please make sure of the current regulations pertaining to the area you wish to fish and by all means buy your fishing license. The best way to find out about the fishing in the area is to ask locals, most are more than willing to give you some ideas. Local sports stores are always great with advice and of course they will be glad to sell you the best lure, spoon or fly to get the job done. If you are too shy to ask most of the guide books on Alaska will give you some hints of places to fish and there are some really great books on fishing in most stores and RV parks.

Grayling are a small freshwater salmonid with a huge dorsal fin. The average length is 8-14". They prefer clear, cool, rocky streams and lakes. Try a small spinner or fly and light gear. They are soft mouthed so don't set the hook hard. If you plan to catch and release, please use a single barbless hook and keep the fish in the water. It is easier on the fish and still gives you the challenge of getting them in the net. By the by they are good eating, fried up fresh. In the spirit of trying out sourdough ideas, I threw together some pineapple, cranberry, pecan muffins to go along with the mess of fish we had for dinner. I

30

used my new silicon muffin pan for the first time. The pan lived up to my expectations and the muffins weren't bad either! We hiked back to Rika and still no bears in sight. After a short drive down the Tok Cutoff (AK route #1) we stopped at a RV camp on Nabesna Road, at the edge of Wrangell St. Elias National Park. After a yummy fish dinner we took the Kick up the road farther and found a beautiful, primitive campsite on Rufus Creek in the park. Our plan was to spend some time in this area exploring and after talking with Thelma, a NP ranger we have decided to move to Rufus Creek for our stay. I don't know why anyone would want to go any farther, after spending time here, it is so beautiful! We are the only ones in this campsite and there really is only room for one more rig to pull in. It is on a gurgling stream, among the black spruce and aspen trees, in the Wrangell St. Elias National Park. We spent 4 days here exploring the area, looking for fish, wildlife and scenery. We did not catch any fish. I guess I am not in the right mood for fishing just now. OK so I'm not a dyed in the wool, got to catch that fish, sort of gal! The big animals are hiding from us too. So far we have spotted nesting Trumpeter swans, some ducks of different types and several varieties of small birds and hawks, a few squirrels and one medium sized animal ran across the road in front of us. We are pretty sure it was a wolverine. What we did see along the way, are a lot of tracks, Wolf, Caribou and Moose to name just a few. The majestic mountains played hide-n-seek in and out of the clouds, the vistas changing moment by moment. It is peaceful and quiet here, the sun and, yes, even the rain was soothing! Thunder and lightning entertained us one afternoon. Not so soothing, that! We hope that it will not start any forest fires today.

An odd thing happened one night not too long ago. I woke out of a sound sleep and started to swat at what I thought was a mosquito buzzing around my ear. It stopped and I went back to sleep only to be awaked again. This time I listened more closely and found that it was Lorrin making the little buzzy sounds while he was sound asleep! Got to love the guy, he is great at imitating wildlife sounds, even in his sleep! As long as he does not start biting like a mosquito, I will be OK!

Wrangell-St. Elias National Park is the largest of all the National Parks in the United States, equal to six Yellowstone Parks. Four major mountain ranges, Wrangell, Chugach, St Elias and Alaska ranges meet in the park and include nine of the sixteen highest peaks in the United States. The Wrangell range is volcanic. Mt. Wrangell's last eruption was recorded in 1900. It is still a primitive place, much the same as when miners first came to this remote land in the early 1900's. Only two roads cut into the park, the Nabesna Road, in the north and the Edgerton Highway/McCarthy Road in the south.

Beaver *[7], [BC, YT, AK, NWT]* & **Wolverine** *[1], [AK] There are folks that live up here all their lives and never see a Wolverine alive, in the wild. We consider ourselves very lucky to have caught even just a glimpse of one! As for the industrious beaver, we saw their dams and huts everywhere we went and were pleased to catch a glimpse of a few going about their daily work. Some of the structures were amazing in size and engineering!*

Grayling

How did Alaska and Hawaii becoming states effect the puppet Howdy Doody? Two more freckles were added to his face, making the number "50", one for each state! So admit it, you remember Howdy Doody, don't you?

Fish wheels on the Copper River, AK

Historic Kennecott mill built in 1907, under restoration today, is a part of the Wrangell-St. Elias National Park, AK

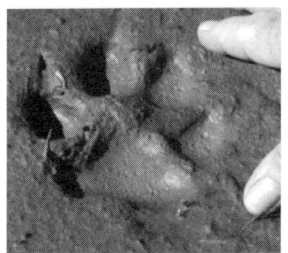

A 5" Wolf track. That is my hand next to the track.

ADVENTURE #6

Day 21-25 Glennallen, AK, - camped * Side trip to: Kennecott, AK - Valdez, AK

We traveled a short distance through snow capped mountains of the Alaska and Mentasta Ranges on our way to Glennallen, our next base camp. In an effort to slow the gas consumption of Rika, our big rig, we are trying to pick central locations and then hub and spoke from camp in the Kick. It gets much better gas mileage and it is much easier to pull into a tight spot for a look see. We have done our pre-planning and know the areas in which we want to concentrate our efforts.

We have reduced our travel costs by staying in State and National primitive camps, with lower costs, alternating with private RV parks, with full hookups. Don't forget to get your National Park annual pass and your senior pass if you are old enough, as these will help give you savings $$. The Alaska State Parks no longer have annual passes available but the fees are not high in the first place. We like the primitive camps as they are often in a more natural setting and often fewer rigs are camped in them. Many times, we have had the camp to ourselves. We do like commercial RV parks as well. It gives us a chance to visit with other travelers, find out where they have been and also we can get local knowledge from camp hosts. It is a nice tradeoff to do some of both and it helps to lower the average daily cost of travel. A word to the wise, it is not recommended that you just pull off at any side road to camp.

Most places are privately owned and without permission you will not be welcomed. Many of the historic pullouts and scenic overlooks are signed "No Overnight Parking or Camping" take heed.

From our base camp, our first day trip was to Kennicott and McCarthy in Wrangell-St. Ellis National Park. It was a long day, but Oh so worthwhile! If we were to do it again, I think we would stay a night at the historic Kennicott Glacier Lodge or maybe one of the Bed and Breakfast lodgings. This way we could enjoy the long summer evening exploring and then the next day make our way back down the road. It is easily a four hour trip each way and we had little time to explore while we were there. There are bush planes that will take you up there and back as well. That might just be a great way to miss the pot holes and washboards and get a great sightseeing adventure to boot.

What/where/why is a Kennicott and McCarthy? [1] the **[what]** they are towns, of the past and [2] they are at the end of a very long, very rough, mostly dirt road in the Wrangell-St. Elias National Preserve, which is in the middle of the Wrangell-St. Elias National Park and [3] it holds a great piece of Alaskan history to say nothing of the vast, picturesque beauty of the drive. Sorry you asked? The explanation seems to bring up more questions, so I will try to answer them all, sooner or later. Let's get the **[where]** nailed down next. From the Richardson Highway (hwy 4) south of Glennallen on the way to Valdez, you will take the Edgerton Road to Chitina, (33 miles paved) and then McCarthy Road to a foot bridge at the end of the road (59 miles of dirt) then you walk or take a shuttle to McCarthy about one mile and Kennicott about four miles farther (25 minute ride one way), are you tired yet? Well, you're not done. You must take time to see each town and tour the sights. Speaking of sights, if you are lucky, as we were, it will be a sunny day, the sights of the surrounding mountains and glaciers are breath taking. Truly one of those places that there are no words grand enough to describe the experience.

Now let's give you some history and some things to look for along the way. As you start up the road you will notice farmland in the Kenny Lake area. It was homesteaded starting in the late 1950's. Continuing along through lush wilderness you come to Chitina and the end of the pavement. Chitina got its start as a railroad town in 1910, providing a stopover for the copper trains traveling between Chitina and the port of Cordova. From here we drove along much of what was the rail-bed for Copper River and Northwest Railway, active from 1911 to 1938. As you cross the bridge just passed the town of Chitina, fishwheels can be seen during salmon runs. They are set along the banks of the Copper River at the confluence of the Copper River and Chitina Rivers. The fishwheels are powered by the river's flow and as the wheels turn, fish swimming upstream are scooped out of the water by wire baskets and dropped into a collector box on the side of the fishwheel for the waiting subsistence fisherman. They are used by Alaskans permitted to harvest fish in this manner. This is a very efficient way of catching salmon to feed their families. The fishwheel has been used in Alaska since the gold rush days when miners set up the wheels to help supplement their diet. McCarthy now serves as a home for guides and others working in the two town sites. It was, in its hay day, a rollicking fast paced railroad and copper mine town, with saloons, pool halls and other forms of entertainment as well as hotels and all manner of stores and shops. While Kennicott the copper mine town, was more family friendly, with a school, dental office, hospital and a recreation hall where dances and entertainment were held. Many of these building are still standing today and there are some really great tours to take to learn the history of the town and the surrounding area. Restoration of the many buildings in town is an ongoing project of the National Park.

And finally the **[why]** is, let's see rivers, lakes, fishing, mountains, valleys, glaciers, wildlife, history, geology and solitude to name just a few. We really love finding places less traveled and this is one great example. If this sounds like a place you want to go, consider these hints. It is a very long day if you do it all in one day. It would have been better to drive up the paved road on the day before and camp at one of the sites along the way. There are also a few B&B's along the road to McCarthy or Kennicott. Do not start up this road without a plan and local knowledge. The visitor's center in Glennallen and south of Glennallen the National Park Headquarters/Visitor Information Center are both good resources for current information. It is highly recommended to have a full tank of fuel, a spare tire for those sharp rocks and "railroad spikes" that you may encounter along the way. Remember you are driving on an old railway. Snacks and water should be taken too. Not only is there no Mickie D's at the next corner, there are a few places at all to get meals and snacks on this trip.

Our next daytrip took us down the Richardson Hwy to Valdez. Everyday no matter how many times I say "this is the most beautiful view ever", the next leg of our trip surpasses the previous one. The drive through the Chugach Mountains is awesome! Worthington Glacier is one of the stunning sights you see along the way. If you look close you might even see the elusive Ice Worm dancing on the glacier. ⚘ Ice Worms are the real thing! Not just in the wild imagination of Robert Service's, "The Ballad of the Ice-worm Cocktail", similar to the earthworm, but just ½ inch long and thin as a thread. They thrive in icy temperatures that would seem impossible for most life. Little is known about their life style. They do not like the sun or heat, preferring to make their appearance at dusk. They have been seen standing upright, waving about in what is thought to be, an effort to catch food such as red algae and pollen, from a glaciers runoff.

You might like to do some salmon or halibut fishing while you in Valdez. I am sure you have heard of highly regarded and ever so tasty Copper River Salmon haven't you?

The town of Valdez is literally surrounded by mountains. ⚘ Valdez is at the end of the trans-Alaska pipeline, where the oil is loaded into tankers for shipment elsewhere in the world. We hope later in this trip to visit the other end of the pipeline in Deadhorse, at Prudhoe Bay some 800 miles north of here.

⚘ Did you know, much of the Port of Valdez was damaged or destroyed by the 1964 Good Friday earthquake and the tsunami in which 33 people lost their lives? Today, the new town is located at a safer site and includes 52 of the old buildings, which were moved from the original site. There is much more to learn of Native American history, explorers such as Captain Cook and Spanish cartographer Lt. Salvador Fidalgo, Russian fur traders, gold seekers and how the town has played a part as a strategic military location for defense and communications.

For something extra special, catch the ferry from Valdez to Cordova and explore this beautiful town with the breathtaking Childs Glacier. Stay for a few days.

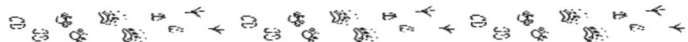

Moose [51], [BC, YT, AK] *I still get excited every time I see one of these great creatures. I could watch them forever! They look so clumsy and slow, but do not let looks deceive! They can be graceful and fast. In a few smooth strides they can go from standing on the side of the road to right in front of your vehicle and don't even think of getting between a mother and calf!*

We saw two Moose, in Two Moose Lake on the Dempster Highway, a mom and calf wading around munching happily on pond goodies.

Why did the moose cross the road?
To see what the tourist was looking at!

ADVENTURE #7

*Day 26-32 Slide Mountain, AK, Glen Hwy - camped * Matanuska Glacier Overlook, AK - camped * Palmer, AK - camped * Side trip to Hatcher Pass, AK*

The Glenn Highway is one of our Nations most beautiful "Designated Scenic Byways." It definitely lives up to its designation! We have taken our time through this area, even retracing part of the highway with the Kick because when we drove through in Rika it was cloudy and foggy, thus obscuring our view of the mountains and valleys along the way. We are so glad that we did, as the beauty of the landscape is spectacular! The sun warmed mountains are so close you feel as though you could reach out and touch their snow covered pinnacles, U shaped glaciated valleys and the braided rivers, born of glaciers, rushing on to the sea. The Wow! factor, to the Max!

This brings to mind something I wrote about what Mother Nature shares with us.

 **SUNRISE**

Have you ever lain upon a hilltop to watch the sunrise?
Wrapped in darkness, you wait in silence.
There is expectancy in the air.
As the minutes pass, a glow peeks over the horizon.
Ever so slightly present
A golden ray sends forth a tentative finger.
With each moment light gathers strength

Stretching out sleepy fingers
Reaching for the heavens
Colors of pink, lavender and gray
Paint the clouds above.
So many shades, changing by the moment
Flashing and moving as if to an unheard symphony.
The music of the sunrise is building
Sending rays dancing across the sky.
Around you, the darkness fades.
The landscape takes shape.
Morning is on its way.
Colors spread across the sky
From horizon to horizon.
Then comes the bright orb
Peeking over the mountains
Pushing back the clouds
Raising slowly bringing light to the sky.
Music can now be heard
As the birds lift their voices to the sun.
The sky has turned to blue with clouds drifting along.
All is draped in golden rays.
Does this bring memories back for you?
If not, make a date with the sun
It will warm your heart
And give you ever lasting memories.

We spent a night in a nice cozy RV camp where we visited with the owners. Their story, like so many up here, tells of coming north years ago to cut a niche for themselves. They have hunted, trapped and labored to make a good life for themselves. You can see they love this land and enjoy sharing it with today's travelers.

The next few nights are spent at a campsite/overlook of the Matanuska Glacier and Valley. It is a busy place as people come and go on their travels. We watch families and individuals stop for a few minutes or over overnight to enjoy the beauty here. We camped in the parking lot (it's allowed here) as we could not bring ourselves to hide in the trees, away from this stunning vista. I sat at my computer trying to describe what I saw as I watched the ever changing panorama of clouds compete with the sun casting shadows and light across valley and mountain. Again my words cannot describe fully what there is here. You must see it for yourself.

I made a loaf of sourdough bread with my starter today. We have not had better and to prove it, I tell you it didn't have time to get cold before the last crumb was snatched up. My sourdough starter and I are becoming friends. I have even given a thought to naming it. OK, maybe that is a little over the top. Remember thou this is from the person that has named the two vehicles in which we ride! OK, OK, I'll give it some more thought (how about Junior) Oops, my bad, strike that thought.

Do you know what makes a glacier? Boy, now that's a hot (no pun intended) topic! Don't expect me to weigh in on the global warming or change debate of today. I do not have a crystal ball nor am I, "all" knowing! So let's stick with facts about glaciers. I have seen my fair share of glaciers all around the world, each one unique in sight, shape and activity. Don't ask for numbers, I could not count them all even if I tried. The bottom line is - snow becomes a glacier when more snow falls than melts continuously, each winter, for a few years. It turns to ice and that ice starts to slip down or out, do to gravity. OK that is very simplistic, but that's all it really takes. I suppose you want more facts, so here is a little information that I have picked up along the way and believe me this is one of those subjects that has many angles, thoughts and conflicting "facts". Everyone writing about glaciers seems to have their own way of explaining the information. There are many different types of glaciers, some hang on the side of mountains, some are covered by deep layers of sediment, called a dirty glacier, others come down valleys ending with their foot in water and still others are gigantic ice sheets that cover large areas of the land's surface such as Greenland and Antarctica. Today glaciers cover about 10% of earth's surface, most laying in the polar regions of earth. During the last ice age, ice covered about 32% of the land and 30% of the oceans. Within the last 750,000 years there have been 8 Ice Age cycles. Glaciers sometimes retreat or advance depending on the amount of snow that falls high up in the mountains above the glacier, each year. When you hear that the ice is retreating, it doesn't really mean that it is moving back up the mountain as the term seems to imply. The ice is still moving down the slope, but there isn't enough snow to replenish what is melting, making it shrink back, giving the appearance of traveling back up the mountain. This is to say the foot of the glacier does lessen but the ice is no longer moving down the mountain, just getting smaller. Glaciers move fast or slow, sometimes you can't see any change over year's and other times they will move rapidly, say 30 feet or more per day. I have seen two glaciers next to each other, one in retreat and the other advancing at the same time, go figure. ⌇ Did you know that in the crater of Mt. St. Helens, in the state of Washington, there is a new glacier growing, the only one to be "born" in my life time. It started some time after the volcanic eruption of 1980. My favorite Glacier is Hubbard Glacier, in Yakatat Bay, Alaska. Some cruise ships visit the glacier on their journeys in Alaskan waters. It is 6 miles across the face, 350 feet tall and 150 feet below the surface of the sea. One can see a lot of activity along the face as ice breaks off (calves) and falls into the salt water making (you got it) icebergs. In 1986, Hubbard Glacier surged across Russell Fjord, trapping water, seals, porpoise and the like, behind the ice plug, forming a large lake. The pressure of the rising water broke the ice dam a few months later. All of this activity is normal and apart of the ongoing climate variation cycle. Did you know that the density of the ice causes it to absorb all light and to reflect only the blue color spectrum, thus giving glaciers their beautiful blue appearance?

Our next few days are spent camped at a RV site near Palmer, doing some needed repairs on the Kick and a little sightseeing in the area. The starter on the Kick has been acting up and as I don't like pushing it to get started every time we want to go somewhere, I thought it might benefit from a new starter. Of course it would only act up when we were far from a repair shop, like on our side trip to the top of Hatcher Pass. Oh well, at least I didn't need to push, all we had to do is start rolling downhill! By the way we really enjoyed the Independence Mine State Historic site, near Hatcher Pass. A side-note for those of you that know, we actually did not make it all the way to Hatcher Pass, as it was still closed for the season and will not open until early July. The mountains around us were playing hide and seek in and out of the clouds. Still we could get a good idea of what the panorama was like from this mining camp, tucked into the cleft of Skyscraper Mountain. We marvel at what these miners had to go through to find gold here. It was hard-rock mining and remote to boot!

It all started here in 1898 with the discovery of placer gold in Grubstake Gulch, near what was to become the Independence Mine. By 1937 the construction of the Independence Mine Camp started and the part time, seasonal mining, became full time. Short lived though, the mine was shut down during WW II in 1943 when it was classified as nonessential to the war effort. After the war ended the mine tried to start up once again but never did very well, due to the low price of gold and internal struggles. The mine was shut down by 1951. Yet in those few years, 181,000 ounces of gold was taken from this mine.

I have mentioned both placer and hard-rock mining. Placer is typically panning or sluicing for loose gold nuggets or flakes in the gravel of stream beds. Placer mining typically came before hard-rock mining. The miners would follow the gold in the streams, up into the hills until they found the gold bearing quartz veins in solid rock. That is where the hard-rock mining came into play. The miners tunneled through solid rock and into the mountain following the gold rich quartz veins to retrieve the gold. And we wonder why gold is so expensive!?

I have been making sourdough goodies and freezing them ahead for our son's visit. So far it has been cheese sticks, chocolate chip cookies, white bread and rolls that I have turned out. The starter has been working very well and is taking on its own unique flavor.

Swans: *Trumpeter & Tundra [?], [AK, YT] I didn't keep track of the numbers we saw along the way. We did see quite a few nesting pairs and goslings as well. The Tundra Swans were in and around Deadhorse. They did not seem to mind all the industrial activity around them as they went about their day searching for food.*

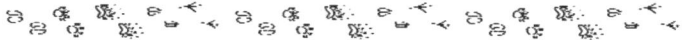

Where else but in Alaska: Roads named! **AT YOUR OWN RISK Dr.** and **WRONG WAY Rd**!

A business sign in Alaska: **"TANNING AND TAXIDERMY"**: What--- you go in for a tan but if you stay under the lights too long, they stuff you and hang you on the wall? Or maybe this is Alaska's answer to plastic surgery?

Fishing in a Portage area lake. Love the reflection!

Animals at the Alaska Wildlife Conservation Center.

ADVENTURE #8

*Day 33-35 Anchorage, AK - camped * Side trip: Alaska Wildlife Conservation Center - Whittier, AK * Portage, AK - camped*

We leave Palmer behind, moving on to a RV park near Ships Creek, right in downtown Anchorage. Ships Creek is world renowned for its premier salmon fishing. It seems a most unlikely fishing spot, right under the tall buildings of Anchorage, where one can take a "fishing lunch break" from work and bring home fresh salmon for dinner. When we checked in we were informed the salmon are slow in coming in this year, but they are catching a few nice fish.

Anchorage, what can I say about this modern, metropolitan city? It has everything, shopping, restaurants, museums, theater, parks, history, you name it and it is here. It's Alaska's largest city with nearly 300,000 living within its boundaries. By the way, that's half the population of all the rest of Alaska! Anchorage got its start when in 1914 when a construction camp was setup as headquarters for the Alaskan Engineering Commission at the mouth of Ships Creek. Cargo ships would anchor in the mouth of the river too off load supplies for the building of a railroad to the coal fields of Chickaloon. The name Anchorage was selected because it was the "anchorage" for ships bringing in supplies for a rail road construction camp at the mouth of Ships Creek. Anchorage's growth came in fits and starts with the building of the rail, then the influx of folks heading for the Matanuska Valley to start a farming community,

WW II and military bases, oil in Cook Inlet and later the North Slope oil fields. These events all played a part in the city's growth. Even the Good Friday Earthquake of 1964 played its part in shaping and growth as a new city emerged from the rubble after it was all but destroyed by the destructive quake.

Did you know 🌲 Alaska has more earthquakes than any other region in North America?

Today it has everything a big city should and yet the wilderness is just outside, with moose and bear walking down the streets of the city on a regular basis. 🌲 Anchorage is considered one of the Air Crossroads of the World, with cargo and passenger flights using Anchorage as a gateway from and to everywhere in the world. Lake Hood and Lake Spenard, next to the Ted Stevens International Airport, is the largest and busiest floatplane base in the world with an average of 235 takeoffs and landings daily. Alaska boasts 6 times as many pilots and 14 times as many airplanes per-capita as the rest of the nation. Many places in Alaska do not have roads going to or from them. Bush planes are the only means by which one can get there.

🌲 Even the Capital of Alaska, Juneau, has no road connecting it to the rest of Alaska, let alone the rest of the world! You must either fly or go by boat to visit this fair city. 🌲 Alaska is unique among the 50 states in that most of its land mass has not been organized into political subdivisions equivalent to the county form of government. Local government is by a system of organized boroughs, much like counties in other states. Some areas are not even included in any borough because of low population in those areas.

The next two weeks are going to be very busy for us. Wayne, our number two son is flying in to spend some "quality fishing" time with us, well maybe some sightseeing too. Number one son and family could not get away from work to join in the fun. Fresh Sourdough Cinnamon Rolls awaited Wayne's arrival. We showed him the sights of Anchorage, tried a little fishing on Ship Creek and then headed out onto the Kenai Peninsula. This area is where they say Alaskans go to play. It has something for everyone. Mountains; ocean; lakes and rivers; world class fishing and skiing; hunting; hiking; wildlife viewing; bird watching; resorts; B&B's and the list goes on and on! We made a stop at the Alaska Wildlife Conservation Center along our way. This is a must do stop, you can get the wildlife pictures you may have missed while traveling and if you are careful you can keep the fence out of the photo and no one will know that you did not see them in the wild. The center does a great service in caring for and rehabilitation of Alaska's wildlife and educating the public.

I'm here to say the Kenai Peninsula is one of those must do areas but you must plan ahead, as it can be very busy at times, especially when the fish are in. We spent a night in the "area" of Portage; a town that no longer exists after the 1964 earthquake. It is nestled in among the Chugach Mountains along Turnagain Arm, just a few miles from Anchorage, yet you could believe you are in a remote wilderness and in reality you are! A side trip to Whittier, with stops at Begich, Boggs Visitor Center and Portage Lake along the way, where ice blue bergs from Portage Glacier bob on the lake. We drove through the Anton Anderson Tunnel to get to Whittier. The

51

tunnel is unique as it is a 2.5 mile, one way tunnel that is shared by trains and cars alternating turns going through. Each direction has ½ hour to get through before the next group is allowed to transit through. The town of Whittier was first constructed as a secret port. The trains were run to safely transport military troops, supplies and petroleum through from the Port of Whittier to Anchorage in support of the war effort in the 1940s. The Army chose this site because it was a deepwater, ice-free port. It was also very difficult for the enemy to locate from the air, making it a safe place for our troops. Before the year 2000, if you wanted to drive your car to Whittier, you had to put it on a flatbed rail car and ride through on the train. To say the least it is a one of a kind place. There are still old military buildings one of which has now been converted into condos and much of the town's population lives in this building. Whittier was originally a self contained community under one roof with a theater; bowling alley; church; clinic; library; post office; stores and more. They were originally used to house soldiers and their families. It even had an underground tunnel so the kids could walk to school, out of the harsh weather of winter. In Whittier today you can catch an Alaska State Ferry, go fishing or sightseeing on Prince William Sound or have a meal at one of the restaurants while enjoying the panorama of sound and mountains. Several the large cruise ship companies port here.

Whittier brings back memories of when I started working on cruise ships. The first few years that I worked aboard, our ships docked in Whittier. It was not much in those days, a few bars, ferry dock, the end of the train track spur and a few boats. It was just a place to get off the ship and head for Anchorage. It has grown some since then. Still here are the mountains and glaciers pinning the town to the edge of Passage Canal on Prince William Sound, where otters cavort.   A place of contrasts, beauty and rubble.

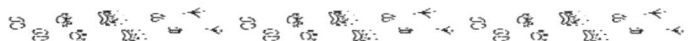

*Sea Otter [5] [AK] & **River Otter** [5] [YT] Sea Otters with their bristly whiskers making them look like old men of the sea. We sat on the beach in Seward roasting hotdogs and marshmallows, watching them swim by bobbing along on their backs and holding their dinner on their tummies. River Otters are clowns, frolicking and romping everywhere they go. We watched one swim around our boat while we fished and another time a family of four lopped across in front of our motorhome, dove into a pond and porpoised across the water so fast we could not keep up.*

A business sign in Alaska: **"CARWASH–LAUNDRY–SHOWERS"**: Do you drive through the carwash with the windows down, the cloths you want washed on the back seat and shampoo in your hair, to get it all done at once?

My 40 # Kenai King!

Wayne's 5 pound Rainbow

ADVENTURE #9

Day 36-41 = Sterling, AK – camped several places

While Wayne was with us we dedicated much of our time to fishing with a little sightseeing thrown in! This is what our son is here for, the sport of fishing, the chance of hooking the "Big One" on the Kenai River, the river of Kings. I had done my homework and found, we think, the best guide service on the river. Big Sky Charter and Fishcamp, Sterling, AK, owner Joe Connors, check out his website at www.kenaiguide.com. After talking and emailing for several months, I decided he sounded like the right match for us. We wanted to fish for Kings, Trout, Charr (Dolly Varden) and do a flight-seeing, fishing, bear watching trip. Joe could set it all up for us and he did. We had an incredible time. The camp was right on the Kenai River situated at one of the best fishing holes on the river. We only had to step into the boat and push off to start fishing. We could see the Kings rolling from shore. They were catching Rainbows, Dolly and Kings off the banks of camp. It was exciting just being there. We could even sit on the deck by the river and watch, who would think that fishing, could be a spectator sport? We had an all day boat trip planed so went to bed early as we were to be on the river bank at 5:30am, ready to fish. At 6am we start fishing, right in front of the camp, very convenient, no long boat ride to the fishing hole. OK, with that big build up, did we catch anything? You know that they call it fishing not catching?

Well, "the story goes like this" and by the way has a mixed

ending. Two Kings were landed as well as a number of Rainbow and Dolly and I won't even talk about the ones that got away or then again, maybe I will. The run has been unpredictable this season and the fish were being fish, didn't want to be caught. At the end of the day, Wayne had landed 2 nice Rainbows 2 & 5lbs. (took pictures and released them) and had lost a big King. The other two fishermen with us had landed one King and several Rainbow and Dolly. As luck would have it, I got the big fish, a 40 pound 42 inch King, (took the picture and KEPT it) also a rainbow pan size and a Charr about 3 pounds (took the picture and released it). The fish that we released were "too big," by regulations to keep. Now, I am not saying that I had the best fishing skills. I got that fish into the boat in spite of everything I did wrong and with the encouragement of our guide, Ryan. In fact I thought I had hooked the bottom at first. I was never more surprised in my life! I'm here to tell you, I'm not the fisher person and I would be willing to bet money I would be the last to catch a fish like that, but I did. Here is the dilemma though, on the one hand, I wanted to shout and jump up and down for the excitement of it all, but felt restrained because Wayne had not boated his fish. He tells me it's OK, that is why they call it fishing not catching, but I still feel mixed emotions. I do not understand, I did everything wrong and caught the fish and Wayne did everything right and his fish got away, it's not fair! It was a great day on the river and it is what memories are made of but I would have given anything to have the story reversed and have Wayne catch the big one, some days are like that. I know that everyone thinks the guide they went with is the best and there are a lot of great guides out there, but I think Big Sky was a good match for us and the camp was a little slice of heaven. Our next big adventure, setup for us by Joe, was a flight to Wolverine Creek, across Cook Inlet, to bear watch and fish for Sockeye. Lorrin, Wayne and I are all going this time. It is a half day trip and it is scheduled for the afternoon. Now if you have been following along, you might remember, I am scared witless of bears, yet here we are heading into bear country, what kind of crazy person am I? OK, I'm not so crazy that I am going to go walking in and around bear territory with bears on all sides of us. I have it well planned, we will fly in to a lake, jump into a boat and stay far from shore! Then while we haul in fish hand over fist, from a safe distance, the bears will pad along the lake and nibble at a fish now and again so we can get those great photos. That is the plan anyway. The area where we are going is not too far away from Lake Clark National Park and Preserve, noted for bear viewing. The ½ hour flight over was great. We spotted bear, moose and Beluga Whales during our flight. If you ever have a chance, make it a priority to take a flight while you are in Alaska! You will get a better idea as to how big and vast and untouched this land is. Every descriptive word you can think of does not come close to matching what you see. When you are up high above the land and sea, looking down, it is a spiritual, mystical event. When we set down it was a bit windy making it necessary to get out of the plane and into the boat quickly to keep the plane off the beach. This was done by walking across a wire at the front of the pontoons. I had a momentary thought of falling in and drifting onto the beach under the nose of a hungry bear. I pushed that thought out and concentrated on not falling in! Dave, our guide gave us the safety talk, the how to fish talk and the guided tour talk on the way to the mouth of the creek. An eagle sat in a snag waiting for fish going up the creek. I am struck again, how lucky we are to be here in such a spectacular setting. There were a few other boats fishing, so we took our place and got busy fishing. Cast and reel, cast and reel, we saw other boats land one or two sockeye and we had a few hook-ups ourselves. We could see schools of fish swim past the boat every once in a while, they just were not cooperating. We moved closer into the mouth of the creek as other boats moved out. I kept one eye on the shore and the other on the fishing. Soon there was a Black Bear splashing along, not even caring that we were near. I took a few pictures and got back to fishing, watching the shoreline more closely now. It is hard to decide which to do fish or watch for bears. Soon our first Brown Bear made its appearance. This bear was not in the least interested in us either. It just wanted to find a fish, just like us. After a few pictures I settled back into fishing, still none in the boat for us. Soon, more boats pulled out and we moved closer to shore again. I now notice that we are in about 1 to 2 feet of water and I start to think that maybe a bear might decide there aren't enough fish in the water and start looking at us as a food source. OK, so I obsess! Blame it on my brothers! The bears came through for us, three Black Bears and nine Brown Bears. This is one of the few places that you can see Black Bears and Brown Bears in close proximity. We also watched a River Otter frolic about our boat, eagles flying over head and moose as we flew to and from the lake. Even the cold wind and rain showers did not dampen our spirits. It just wasn't a fish catching day! Guess we can't have everything. The next day Wayne went out for another full day of fishing on the Kenai, this time no one was catching anything, not even on other boats. Bummer! I want to assure you that it is not for the lack of trying. Both fishermen and guides did everything they could. The fish just did not want to be caught! Having said that how can anyone really complain, when you are out on a beautiful river, in the middle of a fabulous setting, doing what one likes to do? All is not lost. We spend a few days sightseeing out to Homer, a town at the end of a five mile sand spit and we even had the opportunity to enjoy some local "culture" at B J's Bar in Soldotna. Hobo Jim, Alaska's official state balladeer was performing. Many of the songs in his show were written by Jim himself. What a talent. We bought some of his CDs so we could listen to him as we were driving. Many of the folks at the bar were friends of his. He had lived out this way and gotten his start here. It brought us even closer to the Alaskan way of life.

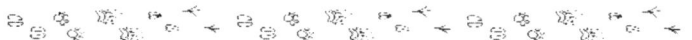

Arctic Ground Squirrel [tons] [BC, YT, AK] these little fellows were everywhere. They are fun to watch as they pop in and out of their burrows, chirping at us. Sometimes they can be a bit too friendly as we found out in Denali NP at the Eielson Visitor Center. If you did not keep a close watch they would try to climb up your leg looking for a treat. The center has just reopened after several years of major renovation. The little rascals had been getting free handouts from the workers. Now the rangers have to retrain them to find their own food. That should be fun! They are very persistent and clever critters.

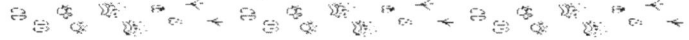

Rika in camp, on the beach in Seward, AK

Fishing along Denali Highway

ADVENTURE #10

*Day 42-44 = Seward, AK - camped * Montana Creek, AK Parks Hwy - camped*

I have always enjoyed the drive down to Seward. I love the scenic beauty of this byway. Our camp was on the beach, at the city park. What a great spot to camp! From here we could enjoy walks on the beach and into town, the surrounding mountains and a campfire in the evening on which we roasted hotdogs and marshmallows. Now that is a meal fit for kings! The fishing was nil right now, so instead we watched sea otters swim by with their dinner balanced on their chests. I have a soft spot in my heart for Seward, another port from my cruise ship days. We drove out to Exit Glacier and along a few other roads that I have not had the chance to explore in the past. Seward is a great little town, population just over 2000 and there are so many must does, visit the Sea-Life Center; go hiking; fishing; kayaking or whale watching, just to name a few activities you can take part in. How about go out to Kenai Fjords on one of the day cruise boats. Check out the marine wildlife for yourself, while you cruise in comfort. If you find yourself in Seward around the 4th of July, you will be smack dab in the middle of Mt. Marathon Race Week. It is a rollicking affair, good times to be had whether you do the run to the top of the mountain and back down yourself or watch from the sidelines. I have only touched on what there is to do here on Kenai Peninsula. You could spend the rest of your life exploring just this one area of Alaska and not see it all.

All too soon we are headed back up Seward Highway, then on to the Glenn Highway connecting with the Parks Hwy near Palmer. Our next goal is Montana Creek. Our hope here was for some Grayling, Lake Trout and Rainbow to catch. Upon our arrival, to our surprise, we were told the Kings were in at the confluence of Montana Creek and Susitna River. Fishing for them would close tonight at midnight. We grabbed our gear and walked the ½ mile to the banks of the Susitna, where the other hopeful fisherman were keeping their fingers crossed in hopes of catching the big one. Time for some good old "combat fishing!" We did see some nice Kings come in, but the fish turned up their noses at what we had to offer. Oh well! It is another beautiful day, so what if the fish were not cooperating with us again. The next day we fished Montana Creek above the highway, a catch and release area. I caught a 14" grayling. Wayne tried his fly rod out. Later we fished Little Montana Lake. As we were walking to the shore a boat came in with their limits in big trout. What a mess of good looking fish! We had spinners and they were biting on worms. Darn! We did get a few bites. The Loons were calling on this peaceful lake and the Mew gulls were crying overhead while eagles made lazy circles in the clear blue sky. By now I am thinking I will not fish any more while Wayne is here. I must be his bad luck penny! I am so frustrated that I am catching and he is not.

During our stay at Montana Creek we also made a side trip into the town of Talkeetna, a must do town. It has the distinction of being the town for which the TV series "Northern Exposure" was fashioned. They have some of the most unique fests, featuring among other events "The Moose Dropping Festival" (no they do not drop any Moose, we are talking of the other kind of droppings, you know what they leave around camp, that you might step in) and a crazy "Mountain Mama Contest" and "Bachelor Auction". By the way, you do know what they say about the men up here? "The odds are good but then again the goods are odd." This little town is also the jumping off point for people waiting to climb Mt. McKinley. From town they will be flown to a base camp, farther up the mountain to start their climb. Sometimes they will wait days on end for a weather window to fly and climb. An average time to climb the mountain is about 20 days.

Did you know that The Mountain was named Denali before it was McKinley? The story goes there was a name swap when the maps were made. The Park was supposed to be named McKinley and the mountain was to stay as named by the Native Americans. The name is an Athabascan word meaning the great one or the high one. It really is the best description of the mountain as it is the tallest mountain in North America at 20,320 feet.

After a long afternoon of sightseeing the homemade Chicken Noodle Soup tasted really good. It is one of my favorite standbys Quick and tasty. The soup goes great with sourdough cheese biscuits. For this recipes check out the "Adventures of Food on the Road" chapter.

Raptor: Eagle, Hawk, Falcon & Owl [?] [WA, BC, YT, AK] We always had an eye trained on the sky watching for our feathery friends. Check out my bird list for which raptors we identified. We saw lots more that we could not identify. My bird book was never far from my reach. My special favorite bird was the Short

Eared Owl. We were fortunate to have the chance of watching as it hunted. What a beautiful bird in flight, dipping and hovering, as it searched the tundra for food.

Here is a dream list for you to check-off

Adventure

Art

Bear Watching

Birding

Boating

Camping

Cruise the Inside Passage

Culture

Eating

Dog Sledding

Fall Colors

Fishing

Flight Seeing

Geology

Glaciers

Gold Panning

Hiking

History

Hunting

Icebergs

Kayaking

Mountain Climbing

Midnight Sun

National Parks

Northern Lights

Photography

River Rafting

Rock-hounding

RVing

Sea Life

Shopping

Snow Sports

Solitude

State Parks

Swim in the Arctic Ocean

Whale Watching

Wildflowers

Wildlife

Wilderness

This is just the tip of the iceberg of what is up North waiting for you. There is so much more waiting out there for you. Just open your mind to the possibilities.

ADVENTURE #11

*Day 45-50 = Cantwell, AK - camped * Mile marker 216 Parks Hwy - camped * Side trip up Denali Hwy*

The Parks Highway takes us north to Cantwell. We made a few stops during the drive to fish some promising streams with good results and a few nice fish. A stop at the Alaska Veterans Memorial is a must do. The Mountain overlook from the park is spectacular on a clear day. We were fortunate to find Mt. McKinley out in all its glory! I am ecstatic, as I have a record to keep! In all the times I have made trips to Denali with my tour groups, they have always had the luck of seeing the mountain at least once while they were in the area. When we arrived at Cantwell to check in, we were told that there is a nice little creek with some fish waiting for us a short distance up the Denali Highway. First thing the next morning we made an early run into Denali Park as far as we could drive, 15 miles to Savage River. We saw a few moose, beaver, snowshoe hare, lots of ptarmigan and The Mountain was out again! Then we drove up the Denali Highway and fished for hours, catching and releasing Grayling and Rainbow. Wayne kept one nice big grayling. I caught two and kept one. This will make a good feed for dinner. We had a good fish fry for Wayne's last night with us and to top it off I made Sourdough Beignets, these are the best treat I could have made for a farewell dinner! They are French, puffy, powdered sugar covered, little squares of tasty heaven. They are also a lot of fuss as they are deep fried and I did them in a small pot, one at a time, all 36! Boy did I enjoy them! Must have been all that hard work that made them taste better than ever!

All too soon Wayne is packing for the trip back. Two weeks flew by in a blink. The weather has been good most of his stay and we showed him a good cross section of Alaska. In the end, he caught a mess of fish, saw some animals and experienced some local culture, saw big city life, Alaska style and wilderness stretching out for ever. To cap off his adventure, he took the afternoon Alaska Rail from Denali back to Anchorage. I think he will come back to Alaska someday soon. The Alaska Railroad is another slice of history that you should not miss. It was built originally to transport coal from the interior to the ships in Anchorage and Seward. Still today you will see coal and other freight on the rail, along with passenger cars loaded with tourists enjoying the beauty of Alaska. It is interesting to note that the construction equipment was shipped to Alaska from the Panama Canal and when the rail was completed in 1923, President Warren G. Harding was on hand, in Nenana, to drive the "golden spike" commemorating the complication of the rail connecting the interior of Alaska, to the tidewater port of Seward.

These last few weeks have been a highpoint of our trip, not only the things we did, but in the sharing of Alaska with someone else, we get more from it too.

Over the next few days we slowdown our pace and ready ourselves for our next adventure, a trip into Denali National Park.

Snowshoe Hare [zillions] [YT, AK] in some areas there were so many of these critters that they had mowed down all the willow bushes in sight. It looked like someone had gone crazy with a weed whacker. They multiply in cycles of about 10 years. As they grow in number they over populate and ravage the vegetation. The numbers of Lynx grow too, supply and demand so to speak.  The story goes that when they chomp on the willow to often something happens in the chemical makeup of the bush and it becomes toxic to the hare. And the population drops back down. Soon the cycle will start over again.

Did you know that Alaska is the only state to share a border with two other countries? Canada and Russia

Wayne did some catching! (Grayling)

Mt. McKinley from Alaska Veterans Memorial rest area.

ADVENTURE #12

*Day 51-57 = Denali NP, AK - camped Riley camp * Teklanika - camped * Bus trip to Kantishna * Riley – camped*

Denali National Park is one of Alaska's top attractions. We have been looking forward to this leg of our adventure for a long time. It has taken a lot of planning and we are anxious to get underway. Denali is the third largest park in the U. S. larger than the state of Massachusetts, roughly 6 million acres of undeveloped wilderness. Unique in so many ways, with few trails and one road, 90 miles long, within the park. Mt. McKinley at 20,320 ft. is the tallest mountain in North America. It is known by many names, Denali, The Great One, The Mountain and of course Mt. McKinley. But by whatever name you wish to call it, you must take time while visiting this park if you want to have a chance of seeing even a small portion of what is here. It is said that about 1/3 of those visiting the park will have the privilege of viewing the mountain. It has a habit of hiding in clouds of its own making. They are created by its great mass and brew up its own weather. You can't just drive through take a few pictures and drive out again. As a matter of fact you can't drive through the park. Most of the road is closed to private car traffic. So how did we get to drive in, you may ask? Plan ahead! That's what we did. There are a few campsites in the "no drive" area and with reservations you, too, could drive in to the campsites. Now that does not mean that you get to do anything you want and drive everywhere you like. There are many restrictions that you must obey. For us it was well worth every rule, to stay 4 nights, (not long enough) 29 miles into the park, at Teklanika River Camp. The rules change as needed to protect the habitat and wildlife. For us, we had to stay a minimum of 3 nights, could only drive in to the camp and out again, one roundtrip only. No driving around while there and we had to leave the Kick in long term park parking outside the no drive area. That may seem a bit over the top but it isn't! The park has a wonderful bus system that will get you where you want or need to go. They are trying to keep vehicle traffic to a minimum for our viewing pleasure and the wildlife's peace of mind. While on the subject of wildlife, most people come to the park to see grizzly bears, moose and The Mountain. Many go away disappointed because their expectations were too high. They are missing the total experience. There is so much more to do and see. First I say, stay awhile, get out of your vehicle and into the wild environment, take in what is around you, listen, breath in, look from the tips of your toes on out to as far as you can see, talk to and ask questions of the people that live and work here. While we were in the park we saw The Mountain; Moose; Grizzly Bear; Caribou; Wolves; Dall Sheep; Red Fox; Hoary Marmots; Snowshoe Hare; Golden Eagles; White Front Geese; Short Eared Owls; Falcons; Hawks; Ravens; a myriad of other birds; Arctic Ground Squirrels; Red Squirrels; Voles...... OK, you get the idea there is so much to see, if you just take the time. I did not even go into the vegetation and bugs.

Yes, by the way, there are mosquitoes. Please do not worry about them. I know you have heard that they are as big a 747 airliner and they could carry you away, but we only ran into large numbers of them in two places in the park and they did not even try to carry us back to their hangar for dinner. There were daily sightings of a Lynx right in camp, though it eluded our eyes. We took pictures of animals far and near, mountains, rivers and flowers. *[Our friends and relatives cringe when we invite them over for fear they may never see all the pictures or maybe they are afraid they "will" see all the pictures!]* Even my fear of bears did not keep me from taking hikes along the river and through the woods. We experienced what Charles Sheldon, a hunter/naturalist/conservationist and Harry Karstens, a guide had the foresight to help establish. In 1917 the Mt. McKinley National Park was established for the protection of wildlife, in particular Dall sheep and the territory in which they roam. Scientific investigation has played an important role from the start. Over the years the park's name has changed to Denali National Park and Preserve. It has been designated an International Biosphere Reserve and has grown, encompassing three times the land and habitat that it once did. Now it covers the complete range of the Denali Caribou herd. The land is still little changed from its beginning.

As you may notice I have a soft spot in my heart for this wonderful example of land use. I could go on and on, but instead I will leave it here and say you must experience it for yourself. All the words and pictures in the world will not prepare you for what you will experience in first person! We will go back again sometime, as we are not finished exploring and we are still looking for that rascal, the Lynx. When you go, remember to join in a few interruptive talks and hikes with the rangers. They will enhance your experience and they are fun too!

Wolf [8] [AK] & **Lynx** [0] my first encounter with a wolf was while I was walking by myself trying to talk some bravery into my heart and mind. I wanted to be able to go for a walk without looking for a bear behind every bush. I had seen Moose and Caribou track on the road but then right in a nice muddy puddle was a very fresh, very large wolf track. It must have been just ahead of me. Hmmm time to go back to the Kick. I did not have to see it in real life, right then. While in Denali we did see seven wolves. One sighting was a mom and four pups. They were a long way off, but we still enjoyed watching them through binoculars, from the park bus. As for the Lynx we did not see one, but we were ever so close! Guess we just have to go back again.

Which state is the most easterly state? **Alaska!** It is also the most northerly and the most westerly of all the states! Well three out of four isn't bad! Check it out!

ADVENTURE #13

*Day 58-61 = Fairbanks, AK - camped * Side trip to Chena Hotsprings*

Fairbanks is our supply stop and respite before we do some real boondocking on the Dalton Highway. We stocked up on a few fresh goods, flour for my sourdough bread project and sugar for jelly making. There will be no grocery stores along the way. We topped off our propane and gas for both rigs, as there will be few places to get gas and no places for propane. Lorrin emptied the holding tanks and topped off the water tank. We also bought an "extra" spare tire for the Kick as two spares are suggested when heading up the Dalton Highway. Did you know that Deadhorse is not the most northern town in Alaska? Barrow is the northern most town. It is only 800 miles from the North Pole. This far north the sun stays above the horizon during the summer for about 3 months starting in early May by, November it sets and does not return above the horizon for another 2 months or so.

We also did some sightseeing in and around Fairbanks It is known as the Golden Heart City. Many travelers will give Fairbanks only a few quick days, thinking that there is little to do here. I find that I never stay long enough. It is said that Fairbanks is the city of extremes. In the summer it can reach temperatures upwards of 100 degrees F and in the winter it can drop below -50 degrees F. It has an arid climate, with an average annual precipitation of only about 11 inches. While there we visited a few of my favorite places, the University of Alaska Fairbanks (UAF) Museum of the North and the Musk Ox Farm. We also did the Discovery Riverboat cruise; drove to China Hotsprings and shopped the Farmers Market. These are only a few of the fun things to do. You could try your luck panning for gold at several places around the area if you are so inclined. Fairbanks got its start, in part, because of the gold discovered in the area. Don't by-pass the wonderfully tasty restaurants of Fairbanks either.

Someday I would like to spend time in Alaska during the winter trying to see the Northern Lights. They can be seen dancing across the sky on an average of 240 nights every year. I dream of experiencing what it is like in the dead of winter to toss a cup of hot coffee into the frigid air and having it freeze into a million tiny crystals before it hits the ground. Just another adventure that I can look forward to someday. Did you know the monthly utility bills in Alaska are among our nations lowest, despite the severe winter weather? This is due to the availability of relatively inexpensive natural gas for heating. Also mild summers eliminate the need for air conditioning. Small compact, well insulated homes and the use of wood stoves for heating are also factors. While on the subject of weather, I would like to say, so far we have had, better than expected weather. Maybe we set our expectations lower than most travelers or maybe it's because we are from Washington State and don't mind the rain, but so far we have not gotten rained out or altered our plans because of bad weather. We have heard that this has been a "bad weather" year with rain every day. Even the dyed in the wool Alaskans are complaining about the bad weather. I bless the cool weather, as I have been here when it is too hot for my comfort! I am not sure what you expect of weather when you think of Alaska, but you will not find snow in the streets of Anchorage during the summer. This is a big state, with everything from 100 F degree temperatures to snow in some places, at any time of year. Don't trust the weatherman to tell you what the weather will be. Just do what the Boy Scouts do, be prepared! So far the temperature range for us this season has been a low 29 degrees F to a high of about 80 degrees F. Not, of course, in one day - thank goodness. While I am busting the weather myth, what about those nasty BUGS up here? You may have heard that the mosquitoes and other nasty flying critters will drive you crazy. You probably want me to tell you when the bug season is so you can stay away during the worst, times, right. Well, I won't do that. Why not, you ask, I thought you were supposed to be helpful? First the bugs are not as bad as you have heard. Second of all they come out at different times during the year, depending where you are; the mosquito season is not the same everywhere at the same time. What do you mean, you ask, it is summer after all? Well think of it as a rolling season that moves north as summer continues. So while it is warm and sunny in Anchorage, Prudhoe Bay is still shaking off the grip of winter. This means the bugs will hatch at varying times depending on where you are. It's that Alaska is bigger than you think thing, again. We have only been bothered by the little biting nuisances a few times and that was only when we were out fishing or deep into the bush. Here is a hint. I was glad I brought the bug nets to wear over our heads. They may look ridiculous on but those pesky critter could only look, not bite! We also had loose fitting cloths and long sleeved shirts. If it was really bad and it never was, we would wear gloves to protect our hands while fishing. Insect repellent is also useful, thou I prefer not to use it any more than necessary, as I try to stay away from chemicals as much as possible. There is always the sport of swatting. I find an electric fly swatter is useful and can be sporting too. 🌲 I learned something, new to me, about bugs. First, the mosquitoes like to stay in the trees, particularly Spruce trees, away from the heat of summer and wind. Second, if you see a lot of dragonflies in an area, there will be lots of mosquitoes and other bugs. That's because that is what dragonflies like to eat. So let's see, don't park your rig in the deep woods and if you see lots of dragonflies, move on! 🌲 Did you know that the dragonfly is Alaska's State Insect? Say what? I bet you thought it was the mosquito! Well it isn't! Go figure! I guess they wanted to honor the dragonfly because it eats those bothersome bugs.

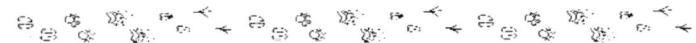

Red Fox [12] [BC YT AK] I had an unexpected encounter with one of these cunning fellows while I was in Whitehorse. You can read about it in Adventure 4. I never dreamed that I would be so close to one in the wild. I have since heard many stories of fox interacting with people in many ways. They have adapted to life near people and seem to be thriving well.

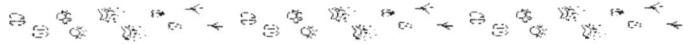

ADVENTURE #14

Day 62-67 = Five Mile BLM - camped * Coldfoot, AK - camped * Arctic Caribou Inn, Deadhorse, AK - stayed * Fairbanks, AK – camped

Our next adventure finds us following the Silver Dragon, the oil pipeline, from Livengood, yes that is the name of a community in Alaska, to Deadhorse, yep, Deadhorse, on the edge of the Arctic Ocean and back to Fairbanks, 828 miles round trip on the Dalton Highway, formally known as the Haul Road. Alaskans have a sense of humor when it comes to their highways. Alaska's highways run from modern freeways to narrow, winding, potholed dirt trails. Some highways are landlocked, so to speak with no connection to any other roads or highways. In the case of the Dalton, Hwy 11, it is paved 25% of the way. That means 555 miles of bone jarring, head bumping, tire popping, gravel road for you and your rig. When we planned this trip, we did our homework. We talked with people that had driven the highway, Alaskans and tourists alike, most would just turn pale, get that glazed look in their eyes and shaking their heads slowly.

They would emphatically say, "Don't do it!" If you want to go, be honest with yourselves, are you capable of changing a tire or taking care of yourself if you get stuck along the way? It is advised that you take extra fuel and two full sized spare tires mounted on rims, as well as a CB radio (there is no cell service along the way) and do not forget emergency supplies. We read up on the route and followed the advice given. This road was built to service the pipeline and is run, mostly by 18 wheelers and heavy equipment as well as hunters and a few brave souls that want to see "what's there." If you "Drive Smart" and follow a few common sense rules of the road you will have a great adventure. Take your time; don't try to do it all in one day. You can't! Read the road as you drive, mud, dust, washboard and potholes are waiting for you. Give the working rigs respect, they know the road and will travel faster than you. When it is safe, pull over and let them pass. Slow down when you see oncoming traffic. This prevents your rig from throwing rocks at the oncoming windshields. You hope that those coming at you will do the same, for the sake of your windshield. Don't stop in the middle of the road when checking out the magnificent wildlife and spectacular scenery, find a safe pull out.

With that rolling around in our heads we set out northbound, hoping that the stories are exaggerated. Just for the record, as a tour director I had traveled the Dalton before, Lorrin had not. The first leg takes us some 90 miles up the Elliott Highway and then on the Dalton, to Five Mile, Bureau of Land Management (BLM) Camp for the night. We are taking our time, catching glimpses of the pipeline and enjoying the beauty of the ever changing terrain, keeping a look out for wildlife along the way. The Fireweed is in full bloom, setting the hills ablaze with color so vividly pink, it is surreal! We crossed the Yukon River on the only bridge in all of Alaska that spans this mighty water. The Yukon River is the longest river in Alaska at 2,000 miles in length, third longest in the U.S. and fifth in North America. We are aware that you do not want to do any funny stuff around the pipeline. Seems that every other vehicle we meet on the road is security, watching to keep everyone on the up and up. They take the safety of the pipeline very seriously.

Our next leg takes us a few miles north of Coldfoot, to the BLM camp at Marion Creek. This will be our base camp. On our walk around camp we have spotted lots of moose sign, our hopes are high that we will see one walking through camp. We will leave Rika here and take the Kick on to Deadhorse. We have crossed the Arctic Circle, done some fishing, (no luck again) and traveled safely to our destination, enjoying every changing moment.

We have done a few must do side trips while staying at Marion Camp, to places like Wiseman, Nolan and Coldfoot. Wiseman is an eccentric, old mining town, population 22, mostly log cabins of varying age and conditions. This was definitely worth the side trip, to see the way life is lived in the bush! Nearby Nolan is a working mine with signs warning that there is danger ahead. We turned around at the sign. The drive was dramatic, winding up hill and deep into the back country, with some great scenic overlooks. Coldfoot, population 13, is a stopover for drivers working on the Dalton as well as tourists in need of fuel, food or a room to sleep. There is also a post office, RV Park and air service to be found. The story goes that the name Coldfoot came to be not because someone got a cold foot while there, but rather for those who gave up and turned around, not going on to the gold fields. On the way back to camp, I noticed that Marion Creek looked like it might be a good spot to try some more fishing. Upon arriving back in camp both the moose and fishing ideas went straight out of the picture, a notice had been posted saying a "¼ mile from camp, in the creek, there was a fresh moose kill." So much for seeing a moose in camp and since fishing next to a dead moose was not on my agenda, I stayed in and baked cookies! The rangers were not sure if it was a bear or a wolf kill. Either way, I was staying close to home! 🫎 We have prearranged our trip to Deadhorse, making reservations for both a room in Deadhorse and a tour of the oilfields. I do not advise going up to Deadhorse without reservations. There are few places to stay and they are often full with the oilfield workers. 🫎 If you want to do a tour of the North Slope, see and swim in the Arctic Ocean, you must make prior arrangements, for security purposes, at least 24 hours ahead. We made our reservations a week out and even at that, we had to change our dates to find an opening in the hotel schedule. It would be a shame if you drove all the way to Deadhorse and could not step foot in the Arctic Ocean!

🐾 The story goes, or so I have been told, Deadhorse got its name from a gravel company doing work on the Prudhoe Bay airstrip of the same name. Why they named the company "Deadhorse Haulers" in the first place seems to be a mystery. So why do the names Deadhorse and Prudhoe Bay keep bumping into each other? Deadhorse is the favored name locally but Prudhoe Bay has the zip code. So this is the way it was explained to me once upon-a-time, Deadhorse is the "city" (the term, city, is used loosely) and Prudhoe Bay is the oilfield. OK, to further confuse you, let me add Deadhorse has only one full time resident and it is a cat! You see the area is in reality an industrial site, not a town. Everyone that works here does so, on rotation. A few weeks working and a few weeks at home, with family, somewhere else, like Fairbanks. They are flown in and out of the site according to their schedule, as a part of their contract. Now do not feel sorry for them being stuck up there in the dead of winter, in a non town, with nothing to do, at the edge of the world. They work 12 hours on and have 12 off. During their off time they have all sorts of activities to keep the workers happy. I am told there are all types of sports, bowling, racket ball, and workout facilities. It is really just a small town, kind-of -sort-of. As for the controversy to do with drilling for oil and all, I will not weigh in on it. The facts, pro and con, are all over the news today and everyone has their thoughts on the subject. If you do make the trip, be sure to book a tour for a firsthand look. I think it was worth our time.

Our third leg north starts early as we want to take our time and still get to Deadhorse in time for our oilfield tour. It was foggy most of the way, making us miss the mountains and vast expanses of tundra as well as just about everything else. At least we could see the road and what was coming, most of the time. We will have a second chance on the way back. As we travel north the trees get smaller and fewer between, until there are no more. We are so far north that trees of any size can't grow in this extreme climate. In fact they have put up a sign pointing out "The Last Tree" on the highway. Sadly someone has killed the 270 plus year old tree, but it still stands proudly for all who pass. The land is now bare mountains and low tundra the rest of the way. We arrive with time to spare, check into the hotel and have a look around.

The accommodations are, what I would call basic, twin beds, in-room bathroom and a TV, that's it folks! I found them comfortable and clean, no complaints. My cell phone even worked while we were in town. When I was looking for accommodations, I found one ad for rooms rather interesting, it stated "Overnight in camp-style rooms consistent with the industrial heritage of the region." Is that a spin or what? We passed on that one. You will be surprised to find that in most cases, there are no restaurants as such, in town. There is however, buffet service at each hotel. There is no need for extra restaurants as the workers are provided with meals as a part of their contract. It is easy for them to get good, hearty meals, quickly. You can check with the hotel for meal times and prices. There is one store in town, The General Store. It is above an auto supply center. I should mention, to be fair, that there are some sundries and souvenirs available at the hotels.

We got to Deadhorse with no flat tires or broken windshields. That is an accomplishment to say the least! Well, OK, we got here before a tire went flat, if the truth be known. A short time after we arrived we found one of our tires going flat. We could not see anything wrong with it. So Lorrin, being the resourceful fellow he is, pulled out the electric tire pump and inflated the tire again. Upon checking it later it was flat again. Darn! After our tour and dinner Lorrin took the Kick to a service shop where it was found that we had picked up a small finishing nail, of all things. Now, we had been waiting for the big blow-out, as we had been warned so often of and come to find out, according to the tire guy, he sees more nails then blow-outs. Go figure! He patched it and all is right with the world!

Our tour took us by oil wells and all manner of equipment and structures to do with getting oil out of the ground and down the pipeline to us waiting at the gas pump, as it were. It was a very interesting tour. We saw Caribou and waterfowl right in amongst the equipment. They did not seem to be bothered by the work and industry going on around them. One of the things we had a chance to do while on the tour is take a swim in the Arctic Ocean. I think about half those on the tour did at least wade in, I being one of those crazy people.

It is said that the water runs a cool 38 degrees F. Believe me it was a quick dip! As for Lorrin, he gingerly dipped his right forefinger into to the water. Where is the fun in that? I even got a certificate to prove that I was crazy enough to jump in.

The sun did not go down while we were here, as it is still summer. Remember the land of the midnight sun! That in its self is something to experience!

Our return trip started early with a hearty breakfast in the hotels buffet line. The tire was still inflated so we loaded up and got underway heading south. The weather was cold and cloudy with some rain showers but it was not hugging the ground as closely as it was the day before. We spotted more caribou near the facilities, along with tundra swans, white sided and Canadian geese, sandhill cranes, snow buntings, jaegers, shore birds and surf birds. Further along a snowy owl and a short eared owl to name a few. Our most exciting sightings were two herds of Musk Ox hanging out close to the road. We had fun watching the calves cavorting around their mothers legs. One group was using the pipeline as protection from the rain. We consider ourselves most fortunate to have seen them at such close range. As we travel along, we start catching glimpses of the Brooks Range. It had been so foggy on the trip up that we could hardly see the hood of our car when we crossed the Continental Divide at Atigun Pass. On our return trip we could see that it was not foggy, instead, it was snowing! Yes, I said snow and there was a lot of it. July 23rd with the Fireweed in full bloom, snow was coming down, what a strange sight, the bright pink blooms covered in fluffy white snow! There was 6-8 inches at Atigun Pass. Luckily it was not sticking on the rain slick road. Our poor Kick was soon covered in mud. They use calcium carbonate to keep the dust down but when the road gets wet it turns into nasty mud that sticks to everything and when it dries, it hardens, making a shell that is almost impossible to get off. I could have made another car out of the harden crust that formed on the Kick. The rest of the trip back to Coldfoot was otherwise uneventful, we did have a better range of sight along the way as the clouds did not obscure as much of the panorama as when we were going north.

We found Rika as we had left her. No crazed Lemmings had gnawed her tires off or anything like that. It was good to get back to our roadhouse, Rika. After dinner we took in a talk at the visitor center in Coldfoot. This is a very nice new, modern building, well staffed with volunteers and professionals, all of which were helpful and friendly, ready to answer your questions. This is an interagency collective with each of the national land agencies working together. You might be interested to know that the highway corridor is federal and public land and it is mostly surrounded by National Park, Refuge & Preserve land. BLM manages what they call the Utility Corridor in which both the road and pipeline run.

The weather had cleared and warmed up for our final leg of this adventure. It was a bit of a long day as we drove all the way back to Fairbanks with a few stops for fishing and Fireweed blossom picking. I have wanted to try my luck at making Fireweed jelly, so we watched for a safe place to park and pick. We were surprised at how quickly the flowers had changed. They had been in such profusion just a few days before and are now only somewhat pink. We found a fair area and got to work plucking buds and dodging bees. Fireweed as the name implies, is the first vegetation to grow after a forest fire. It is a hardy plant that helps the land naturally recovery from the ravages of fire. Because we only want the flower petals, no stems or leaves and it takes 8 cups of these tiny little flowers for a batch of jelly, it took some time to gather enough to fill out the 8 cups. Back in Fairbanks and after a quick meal I got to work on the jelly. Well, OK, as it turned out it did not set completely.

"The syrup" will be good on pancakes. There is a legend about Fireweed that says it is the foreteller of winter's arrival. As its single stalk reaches skyward throughout the summer, first to come are the long thin leaves. As the summer progresses the stalks grow taller and small pink floweret buds start to appear along the upper portion as the stalk continues to reach for the sky. The lowest floweret open first and then each successive bud opens along the stem all the way up to the tip, as the last pink petal fades and seeds start to from a cotton-candy like top, winter is soon follow. The legend really seems to work too. The summer season varies so much due to the elevation and how far north you are, that you can't say winter starts at any one time. So by watching the plants cycle you can tell you how soon winter will arrive at any particular place. What I think is interesting, is that the farther north and or the higher in elevation you go, the plant does not grow as tall, due to the shorter growing season, thus allowing it to complete its life cycle more quickly and fulfilling the legend.

As for the rest of the trip down the road we had no more trouble with our tires but we did take a few small dings in Rika's windshield just before we reached the pavement. As luck would have it several private vehicles did not follow the rules of slowing down for oncoming traffic. It takes just one careless driver and the rocks fly. The road over all had less traffic then we expected and it was better than folks seem to think. Yes, the big rigs are rolling, but they all are polite slowing down and keeping to their side of the road and most of the private vehicles followed the rules too.

Muskox (Musk Ox, Musk Oxen, Muskoxen, I have seen it written all these ways so you pick) [40ish] [AK] these creatures from the Ice Age are so unique, it was a special treat to get an up close view of them. Muskox were hunted to extinction in Alaska in the late 1800s and then reintroduced in the 1930s, brought in from Greenland. The herds are growing in numbers.

Muskox with pipeline overhead.

A **"for real"** sign in the Wiseman Trading Post, a **"for real store"**: If you see something you want to buy put the money in the jar. If you don't have the right change, step out onto the porch and yell **"8 Ball!"** It did not tell us what would happen next though!

ADVENTURE #15

Day 68-75 = Big Delta, AK, (Rika's Roadhouse) - camped * Chicken, AK - camped * Dawson City, YT - camped * Side trips to: Bonanza Creek, Midnight Dome & Dempster Highway/Tombstone Park

We must start heading east and south now as the summer is soon to end and our adventure will be winding down. Before we leave the fair city of Fairbanks we had the windshield patched, hoping to prolong the life expectance of the windshield. Due to the late morning start when leaving Fairbanks and the few stops we made along the way, one at Delta Meats for some reindeer sausage and at Delta Junction for a photo shot at the end of the Alcan Highway. It may be the north end of the Alcan Highway but we have to reach Tok before we will have traveled all 1,422 miles of the Alcan.

We made a short hop today, as we wanted to stop at Rika's Roadhouse in Big Delta State Historic Park. As I stated earlier in the book, this is the roadhouse for which we have named our motorhome. Roadhouses were built as waypoints along major transportation routes throughout the north, providing a comfortable place for early-day travelers. It is still as nice as we remember, green lawns, old log buildings and the river. As we pass through Tok we found that they are experiencing a Spruce Bark Beetle infestation this year. You can see the creepy big beetles everywhere. I have heard many explanations for why the Spruce Bark Beetle has infested some of the forests in

Alaska, Yukon Territory and British Columbia. In the past we were told it was an insect from overseas, brought in by foreign plants, that and other ideas that are now thought to be wrong. I have now learned that this beetle has been in these forests for millennia. They are a part of the natural forest cycle. Normally they are a healthy part of the forest, controlled by small mammals and insect loving birds. Hot summers and mild winters, along with the lack of a "normal" forest with spruce trees of all ages growing together, are factors of an infestation. Although seeing the dead and dying forests may worry you, think about the fact that changes in forests have always been a part of the life cycle and it will continue to do so on into the future. As these changes occur in the forests, different vegetation will take the spruce trees place and even the wildlife of the spruce forests will be replaced by different mammals and birds better suited for the new growth. Or maybe some act of nature, such as a very cold winter, will kill the beetles back to a normal population and the forests will recover. Only time will tell.

Moving on, we head for Chicken. Yes, that is the name. It got its start with gold as so many other towns up here and they are still digging gold out of the ground today. In its hay day there were about 400 residents living in the area. You may wonder why name a town Chicken? Well the story goes, the miners survived the long cold winters by eating a lot of Ptarmigan, (the P is silent) a grouse-like bird. They wanted to honor the bird by naming the town Ptarmigan. The dilemma came when no one could spell the bird's name. Someone decided that it tasted like chicken and the name stuck. The town also has gained some fame because of the book "Tisha", written by and about a young woman, Ann Purdy, who came to teach in the town of Chicken, during the gold rush. The year round population in Chicken is now five, three of which includes the postmistress and her family. Now that is a close knit town! It explodes to upwards of 300 in the summer with all those miners hoping to strike it rich. During our stay we were treated to several of the most stunning, brilliant, double rainbows that we have ever seen. Maybe we should be looking for the pot of gold instead of nuggets!

The folks I have met along this highway, living deep in the wilderness, make me think how different life, even today, would be, in this land of midnight sun and long winter darkness.

 ## It's a Different Life up Here

Some go to find themselves.
Others, to get lost.
Some come for the adventure.
Others just want the quiet solitude.
They come to strike it rich, to hunt & fish.
Others, to soak in nature around them.
Some come for what is in the present.
Others, to find the stories of time gone by.
They come to build roads, pipelines and more.
Drawn by the promise of good paying jobs and good clean living.
They come just to visit, never to leave, putting down strong
*   roots.*
The land up here will get a grip on you and never let you go.
Everyone that comes into this land has a story of their own to
*   tell.*
There are those that dream of coming and never do.

Of those that do make it up here, not all will stay, deciding, this
  life is not for them.
It isn't for everyone, you know.
If you decide to give it a try,
Throw off your old life and learn the ways of the North.
Or you'll never fit in!

As I stated, the town of Chicken is what you would call, small, as towns in Alaska often are. Yet we have a choice of several RV camps with electricity and Wi-Fi to boot. The electricity is from a generator and the Wi-Fi is satellite. Even way out here we can find the comforts of home! Something that you may not know is that many of the private RV camps in the Great North are current on providing us with amenities. You can reach out to those you left at home, telling them of your adventures and sending those great photos as it happens. Still there are many areas that you have no cell service at all so the computer is the next best thing to talking with them. I am going to check out phone service through the internet. I have heard from several fellow travelers that have done it and they say it works well. It is so peaceful and relaxing in Chicken, we spend several days going for walks and just kicking back. Lorrin even tried some gold panning in the creek. Guess I will have to wait for that gold nugget paperweight awhile longer! He spent the day in the creek with not one tiny flake to show for all his back breaking work. Those campers that stay for more than a day are here to strike it rich. Many have sophisticated gold mining equipment and spend every day out in the trenches. Several large nuggets have been found here in the last few days.

Our plan was to set off across the Top of the World Highway in the morning but the rain changed our minds. For the first time all summer, we have held off an extra day because of weather. It was socked in and raining. We found that it was no hardship to stay another day, at the end of the rainbow, as we were in hopes of grand vistas for the next leg of our trip. This proved to be a good decision on our part, as the next day's dawning was beautiful. The rain had stopped, the fog was lifting and the sun was peeking out as we hit the road.

This was the first time we have traveled the Top of the World Highway and are anticipating a beautiful drive. We always try to read up on the area before we drive, new to us roads. We ask people that have just been on the road about the conditions of the road and what will there be along the way to see and do. We also check other sources such as local Visitor Centers and online, giving us better knowledge for making our choices. Then we make up our own minds as everyone will have their own opinion of what it is like to drive the highway in question. About this highway, we have been told that it's brutal and just like the Taylor Highway, (whatever that means), others have said just the exact opposite. We find as always, the truth, for us, is somewhere in the middle. If you are not used to driving on dirt roads and in the bush, far from civilization, you may be uncomfortable and uptight. If it has been raining for days on end, it will be muddy and all you will see are the potholes. If it is cloudy you will not see the sweeping vistas and vast expanses laid out before you. If it has been hot and dry it will be dusty and you will hit washboard ruts. If the caribou are hiding on the other side of the ridge you will think that there are no animals to be found. The bottom line is, take your time. By waiting an extra day we had fair roads, the beauty of mountains and valleys that seem to go on forever and yes, we saw a heard of caribou. Yes, we found mud, dust, potholes and washboard ruts too. Just slow down. If someone is pushing you, pull over and let them by. If someone is coming at you in the middle of the road pull over in the widest spot available, without going too far to the side, watching out for soft shoulders and stop. This way you are in control, making them, pass you. I say again take your time. Don't make the drive a forced march. You are on the vacation of a life time, enjoy it. If you get tense find a pull out, stop, take a walk, pick some berries, go fishing or take a nap, enjoy the view. You will soon be smiling again and ready for the road. Some people do not heed this advice. We passed by a car in the ditch, on its top, near Boundary. When we asked about what had happened, we were told someone was trying to get to the border before it closed for the night. Guess he did not make the crossing. Luck for him he came out of the wreck better then the totaled car, with only a few scratches, bumps and bruises. Make sure you check out Boundary on your way, it has some very photogenic log cabins. It is said to be one of the earliest roadhouses in Alaska.

I believe that the Top of the World Highway has some of the most beautiful panoramas in the world! I know, I know, I say that about every road we have driven, but this time it is really true, really! I find myself saying "Unbelievable" over and over again. The road follows ridgeline after ridgeline until you truly believe that you are on the top of the world! The highest elevation on the road is only 4,515 ft. You are above the tree line and just like the song says, you can see forever! OK, for the record I am certifiably hooked on the Great North and I think it is all the best, most, grandest, wonder-fullest...OK, do you get it now? I am in my Shangri-La and loving it! We stop often to take in the scenery that surrounds us. Sometimes this is the only time the driver can take his or her concentration off the road and see more than just what's ahead. All too soon we drop down to the Yukon River and board the George Black Ferry across to Dawson City. Now, you do not find many things in this world today that are free, but this ferry is! It is also small, taking only a few vehicles at a time. Between the time of spring breakup and when it freezes up in the winter the ferry runs 24/7, with a few layovers for maintenance and fueling. The rest of the year you can drive across the river on the ice if you like!

Ahhh, Dawson City, what a unique town, right out of the past! False front buildings, dirt streets, honky-tonk music drifting out of Diamond Tooth Gerdies and down the streets. This town will get a grip on you and yank you right back to the late 1800's. You may expect to see a miner with his bag of gold sauntering down the street with a cancan girl on each arm and you just might, as there are often folks dressed in period costumes giving talks and shows. Names like Jack London; Robert Service; Arizona Charlie; Martha Black and Pierre Berton are entwined with this town's history. This is where gold fever was at its height. Today, you can still strike it rich in the gambling hall or the streams nearby. Play a one armed bandit at Diamond Tooth Gerties Gambling Hall. If you lose there, it is OK, the money helps in the upkeep and restoration of this historic, gold rush town. Did you know, Dawson City is the only place in all of the Yukon in which you can gamble? Revel in the history of its many museums, for that matter the whole town is a museum! Join in a reading of a Robert Service poem while sitting by his cabin. "The Cremation of Sam Magee" will come to life for you. The town is just the beginning of the fun. We drove up the hill, behind town, past cemeteries, where if you look closely, you just might see shadows of the past hovering nearby. Our destination is the top of Midnight Dome. From here, if it is clear, you can see the confluence of the Klondike and Yukon Rivers, Dawson City and far beyond. Nearby, you can pan for gold in the same creek where the frenzy for gold erupted when George Washington Carmack, Skookum Jim Mason and Tagish Charlie found the first yellow metal nuggets. It was called Rabbit Creek then, now called Bonanza Creek, named after the first claim of the same name.

Claim number 6 is free for you to try your luck if you like, so bring along your gold pan. Don't do any claim jumping though, as it is a very serious offence and you could get shot! In the afternoon we took the free ferry back across the Yukon River and walked along the river to the riverboat graveyard where you can still make out the skeletons of three riverboats among the trees and brush. Many years ago they had been hauled out before winter freeze-up and never returned to ply the river again. The stories they could tell, of their many adventures on the rivers of the North Country, if only they could. We were surprised by a raven black fox that jumped out in front of us as we drove back to camp. It scampered away before I could get a photo, oh well!

We took a full day, boat trip, 100 miles each way, on the Yukon River to Eagle, AK and back to Dawson City, traveling in comfort on Yukon Queen II, a jet boat that runs the waters between the two towns. It is a fascinating trip through history and wilderness.

We spent the next day driving the Kick along the Dempster Highway through Tombstone Park. The Dempster was officially opened in 1979, the only all-weather Canadian highway to cross the Arctic Circle. Although we did not travel the full distance, 456 miles to Inuvik, NWT, we did take the full day going as far as we could (110 miles, one way) and still get back without running out of gas! The real beauty of the area opens up as you reach the parks information center. A stop here helps prepare you for further travels along the highway. They were just putting the finishing touches on a new Visitors Center. The change will be dramatic, from a tiny 10' by 25', information packed hut, to an impressive 2 story structure with a welcoming entry to greet all who come by for a visit.

The many viewpoints will take your breath away as you travel through mountains, valleys and vast expanses laid out before you. Stop for awhile at Two Moose Lake, maybe you will see two moose in Two Moose Lake, we did.

As I have said before, even though it is called a highway, it is not the nice, smooth, paved, four lane highway that you are use too back home! Most of the highway is unpaved and there is an abundance of tank traps, pot holes and gravel. It is sometimes narrow, dusty and muddy. High adventure awaits you but don't let that stop you! It's worth every bump to see what few have had the pleasure to experience. There is a diverse abundance of wildlife to watch for, of which we saw some. I again remind myself, this is a big land and the animals easily hide themselves from our searching eyes! One must keep an eagle eye on the terrain all around and your persistence may be rewarded! If you go, do so prepared and you will have a great adventure! Our time in Dawson City has been all too short.

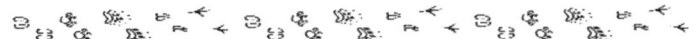

Caribou *[45] [BC, YT, AK] we never saw the vast herds flowing across the tundra as I hope someday to see. While traveling the Top of the World Hwy, just across the border into the Yukon, we did spot a nice group of about 20 or so, far off, standing on a windswept ridge, in hopes the wind would blow those pesky bugs away from them. They were a part of the Forty Mile Herd that frequents the area. With the binoculars, we could see that they had the most magnificent antlers that we had ever seen! Their silhouettes were stunning.* Did you know? *[1.] There are twice as many Caribou in Alaska and the Yukon than there are people, [2.] Reindeer and caribou are only different because caribou are wild and reindeer are domesticated [3.] They are the only member of the deer family that both males and females have antlers. [4.] Horns and antlers are not the same, if you were wondering. Horns continue to grow year after year and antlers are re-grown annually.*

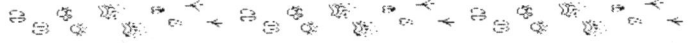

The remains of one of the sternwheelers near Dawson City, YT

Wyatt Earp sailed north in 1897 during the Nome gold rush. He owned and ran several saloons and gambling houses.

ADVENTURE #16

*Day 76-82 Mayo, YT - camped, Side trip to Keno, YT * Carmacks, YT - camped * Faro, YT - camped * Overnight side trip to Mad Mike's, cabin, Canol Rd * Mad Mike's home, Ross River - camped * Francis Lake YT - camped * Watson Lake, YT – camped*

This week's travels are really several unplanned back to back adventures that we just happened to stumble upon! The first deviation is to Mayo and Keno up the Silver Trail. I have often gone by the turnoff that leads to these mining towns and wondered what was up the road. When Lorrin asked me about what was there, we looked at each other and the next thing you know we were on the way to new discoveries. We found a wooded campsite near Mayo and parked Rika on the banks of the Mayo River. Mayo, unlike many towns up here that got their beginning from gold and later silver, was instead, a river port for the shipment of ore to Whitehorse in the early 1900's. Today Mayo still functions as a base for mining exploration in the area.

From Mayo we took the Kick up the rest of the way to Keno in the afternoon. Most of the road is gravel and a little bit bumpy. Again, we find much to enjoy as we wind our way through deep valleys up into the mountains. Keno is a funky little old mining town, nestled into the mountains that surround it. Today it is populated with a small number of miners, artists and long time residents. Many old buildings stand proudly as a reminder of a grander time. We were given a warm welcome at

Jackson Hall, the one time Community Center, now housing the Keno City Mining Museum. This building had first been a hotel in Dawson City then in the early 1920's it was moved and rebuilt in Keno City. We had a look around and found this building and the other outlying buildings to have a plethora of interesting photographs, information and memorabilia dealing with the town, mining and the surrounding flora and fauna.

During our journeys when visiting historic towns like this one, we look for "Walking Tour" pamphlets to help us get the most out of our visit. The booklets published by Yukon Tourism and Culture are some of the most informative available and they are free to boot! In the Keno booklet we found information about the Keno Hill Signpost and could not resist checking it out, just 6.5 miles up the road, to the top of a mountain. We were told that it was a nice walk. Oh sure, 6.5 miles straight up! Or if you like, the road was passable to drive, it was, just. Oh what panoramic views we had from the top, of the McQuesten River Valley and the Ogilvie and Wernecke mountains and of the silver claims doted out across the valleys below! It was worth every bump, getting to the top. You can drive right to the signpost elevation is 6065 feet. Each arrow on the signpost represents the country from which a scientist came to attend a conference in Keno, during International Geophysical Year, in the mid 50's.

You may be wondering about the names of these towns.

The stories go, originally Keno City was named Sheep Hill by the miners. It was later changed to Keno City for a silver claim of the same name. The claim was named after a game of chance popular throughout the early west. Mayo was named for Alfred

Mayo, a steamboat Captain on the Yukon River. Mayo has a very nice Interpretive Center and Binet House Museum was worth our time. We were glad to have taken this side trip. Glad too that we had the time and flexibility to alter our plans for opportunities such as these.

The driver-guides I have worked with have a story they tell their passengers as they pass the turnoff to Mayo.   The story goes something like this: We mustard pass the Mayo turn.   They won't lettuce tartar or we will be in a pickle. If we stop, I do not relish the catsup later. Don't stew about it, as you know this is my bread and butter, so don't put me in a jam! We call that a "Groaner" or otherwise a "driver joke" in the biz!

We spent the night in Mayo and a night in Carmacks before we made our way on to the Campbell Highway (YT 4). Ahead of us was 362 miles of mostly unpaved road. We spent one night in Faro at a nice municipal camp with a wonderful visitor center and then on to our next impulsive adventure. Our plan had been to get fuel, in Ross River 7 miles up the North Canol Road, have a look around and drive on. We drove to the edge of Pelly River in the town of Ross River and found a cable ferry crossing and a foot suspension bridge.   To keep things straight, the story goes like this - Ross River, the town of, used to be on the other side of Pelly River where Ross River, the river, joins the Pelly River and the suspension bridge over the Pelly River, once held the oil pipeline out of the waters of the Pelly River, they moved the town of Ross River to the other side of Pelly River and there is no longer a pipeline, but the bridge is still there. Well is that clear as mud? Being the curious types, we wanted to know more about what was on the other side of the river. We asked the ferry operator, "Mad Mike" (yep that's his name) if we could park Rika at the landing and take the Kick across for a short drive up the road to see what there was to see. It was about 11:00 am, the ferry shuts down for lunch at noon, starts again at 1 pm and stops for the night at 5pm. After a short talk with Mike, we found that the road is really rough, long and the scenery doesn't open up until one drives about third of the way up the Canol Road (50ish miles) to what he called "up-top", meaning the other end of the road. There wasn't enough time to drive up and be back before the last ferry. We chat some more, trying to decide what to do. One thing lead to another and the next thing we know, we had parked Rika at "Mad Mikes" house, taken the Kick, loaded with supplies, across the ferry and are heading "up-top" where we were given directions to his trapper cabin. He even lent us a gas can so we would have enough fuel for the trip. Our plan was to stay one night at his cabin and return the next afternoon. Mike told us that if we were not off the road in three days, he would assume we were in trouble and he would come looking for us. I am still not sure how all this came about, but we had a great adventure along the way. The Canol Road is described in "The Mile Post" as maintained to "minimum" standards, possibly the most understated description of any road, ever! This road is not to be taken lightly. This is the north portion of the WW II oil pipeline and supply road, 144 miles, one way for the part we did, now a National Historic Site. We spend the afternoon exploring the road, its history and its magnificent beauty, then found Mike's cabin without a hitch, with the help of his hand drawn map. All the comforts of home awaited us and for a bonus, a fabulous view of mountain and glacier. Who could ask for more! We laid out our sleeping bags, ate dinner and turned in for an early night. We only had one visitor during the night. I am still not sure what it was, but it didn't sound very big, not like the Grizzly Bear Mike told us watch out for. We were soon back to sleep after it stopped scratching around in the wall and settled down, that is. In the morning we looked around, but the creature never showed itself. With the weather holding, we made our decision to continued north on the road, a distance of about 30 miles, to the Northwest Territory Board. This is not the end of the road, as it continues on from the border another 230 miles to Norman Wells in the Northwest Territories, on the Mackenzie River. From the border onward, it is called the Canol Heritage Trail. It is truly no longer a road, just a trail and not maintained. It is not recommended for vehicle travel beyond the NWT border as there are many washouts and other hazards. It is even difficult for hikers. By-the-by the pipeline originally sent oil 500 plus miles to Johnsons Crossing and on to Whitehorse to help support the war effort. In total only about one million barrels of oil were pumped before the war ended in 1945 and the project was abandoned. There is little left to be seen of this project, as most everything has been salvaged and scavenged over the years, yet there are many glimpses into the past, if you take time to look for them. The upper section of road is exceptional, especially Macmillion Pass, a narrow cut with steep mountains ushering you along. All too soon we must start our return trip, back down the road to Ross River. There is so much to see along the way, spectacular mountains, wildlife, rivers and lakes, WW II truck, bone yards, remnants of the pipeline, even a wrecked WW II Twin Pioneer aircraft can be seen from the road. Today there are several modern mines, lead, zinc and uranium, in operation along the road. We retraced our tracks 144 miles back to the ferry making stops along the way for pictures and to take in all that surrounds us.

Mike was pleased to see us safe and sound. We gave him a report on his cabin and the road, as he had not been there in a few weeks and then we invited him to our motorhome for dinner. The evening was spent swapping stories with Mike and sharing our meal of King Salmon. By the way, the southern Canol Road from the Campbell Highway to Johnsons Crossing on the Alaska Highway is not recommended for travel. Before you attempt any part of this road north or south, check locally about the conditions, as they change daily! Ours was a one in a million adventure! The stars and planets must have been aligned to give us the optimum experience! We were very lucky and thanks to Mike, it all worked out to be one of our top adventures. If you go I hope you will meet someone like Mad Mike for your own adventure.

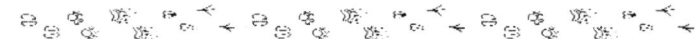

Willow & Rock Ptarmigan and Spruce Grouse [#?] [YT, AK] *I did not try to count them all. As for Ptarmigan, we saw large numbers. They were entertaining to watch and we got lots of nice close-ups, as they were very photogenic. My all time favorite was Mr. Spruce Grouse. When we were driving through "Mac" Pass on the Canol Road, he stepped out in front of the Kick and would not move out of the way. First, strutting his stuff, then flying a short distance, only to land in front of us and again fanning out his tail feathers and flashing his eye patches, prancing around to our delight. What a handsome fellow! He entertained us in this way for several minutes and yes, I got pictures.*

Willow Ptarmigan

Keno Hill Signpost 6,065′elev.

WW II truck bone yard on the Canol Rd. YT

How big is Alaska? It is so big that you will never see it all even if you live to be 200 years old!

How big is Alaska? It is so big the wildlife gets lost in it!

How big is Alaska? It is so big that it will even make a Texan feel small!

Walkway and Brown Bears at Fish Creek Wildlife Viewing Area, Hyder, AK

Salmon Glacier on beyond Fish Creek Wildlife Viewing Area

ADVENTURE #17

*Day 83-92 = Dease Lake, BC - camped, side trip to the town of Telegraph Creek BC * Stewart, BC - camped * Telkwa, BC - camped * Prince George, BC - camped * Lac La Hache, BC - camped * Nairn Falls Provincial Park, BC – camped * Border crossing, Blaine, WA * Home*

Our only "planned" stop on the Cassiar Highway (#37) was to be a side trip out to Hyder, AK hopefully to see some Brown Bears. Being that Hyder was a long ways down the highway we made an interim overnight stop at Dease Lake. The camp we choose was nestled in the pines, next to a rushing river. We visited with some folks that we have bumped into several times along the way. They mentioned that they might drive out to the town of Telegraph Creek in the morning. The next morning we headed on south, but not for long. Lorrin asked me what was interesting to see along Telegraph Creek Road. Not knowing anything about the area, I got out the information and read it to him. The main points read like this; it is 70 miles one way; follows an old telegraph route into gold country and through the Grand Canyon of the Stikine to a late 1800's gold rush town. It is rough and gravel; with 18 to 20% grades (steep) with switchbacks; it runs along the side of cliffs in some areas and on a spine or ridge with very deep canyons on both sides in other parts! I wonder, was it the 18 to 20% grades or the very deep canyons with switchbacks that got his attention? Whatever it was, the brakes were applied and back we went to the same campground we had stayed in the night before. 🙏We dropped off Rika and packed the Kick for a 70 mile must do trip up Telegraph Creek Road. I must say the road was gravel, but not rough at all. They have been doing some roadwork making it the best gravel road we have been on all season. As for the rest of the description, it was all very true! Steep; switchbacks; cliffs; ridge tops; canyons all there, waiting to take our breath away in more than one way! It is so different from all the places we have visited this summer, WOW! Even though we are less than 100 miles from saltwater, it is dry and arid, with juniper and pines, open range and volcanic rock formations. The town of Telegraph Creek has changed little from the early 1900's, when it was at the head of navigation for riverboats on the Stikine River. One of the historic buildings still standing was once a Hudson's Bay Company Post, built in1898. It is still in use today as a café, store and lodging. Once again we have found a way to travel back in time, giving us a glimpse of what it was like during the pioneer days, when thousands of stampeders heading for the Klondike and other gold-fields, streamed through this area. This is only the resent history of which I speak, for centuries before the first European, Robert Campbell, arrived, the Tahltan, First Nations People, fished and hunted this land and still do today. All too soon we retrace our path back to base camp with another adventure under our belt.

Stewart, BC and Hyder, AK will be our next stop. That's right; we will be in Alaska again and another must do stop. Even though we have traveled for days through the Yukon and Northern British Columbia, we still have not gotten below Alaska's panhandle. The tiny towns of Stewart, BC and Hyder, AK are at the tip of a peninsula, tucked in behind Misty Fjords and Tongass National Forest, not far, as the crow flies, from Ketchikan. To get to Hyder from the Cassiar Highway, you drive the 40 miles southwest on highway (#37A) to the town of Stewart, BC, then cross the Canada/U.S. border and there you are smack dab in the middle of Hyder! OK, so Hyder is not what you would call a metropolis. On a good day there may be 100 fine folks living in this funky little town. I believe there are more bears in the woods surrounding town than residents living here, that is, unless you count all the tourists, many of which come here year after year to see the bears, during the salmon run.

Stewart is the "big" town weighing in at population 600ish, also fine folks to be sure. Historically these towns started out, you guessed it, as gold rush towns. Today mining is still present, logging and tourism round out Stewart's and Hyder's economy. These towns are snuggled into the base of majestic, glacier crowned mountains on the Portland Canal. While we were there it was foggy and rainy, no big surprise as they are located in a temperate rainforest! We had come to do some bear viewing at the Fish Creek Wildlife Viewing area. I know, I know, what was I thinking? With my bear phobia, why would I put myself in the woods with bears, yet again! Yes, I still have heart palpitations just thinking about bears but I love seeing them too! Is that crazy or what? It is fascinating to watch from the observation walkway as the bears splash along the river looking for a fish to catch. The knowledgeable staff gave me the comfortable feeling of safety, well as much as possible in an environment where bears come and go as they please and humans are kept in line by very strict rules. I am not sure if the rules are there to protect the humans from the bears or the bears from the humans. The bottom line is bears don't read signs, so I guess we should! In any case, I felt safe and the bears didn't seem to worry about all those cameras clicking while they happily munched away on fish! We did get up close and personal, not by my choice, to one Black Bear. On the first day of our visit to the park, we were walking back to the Kick. I stopped at the end of the walkway, at the gate and very carefully looked both ways and all around, no bears, good! I opened the gate and started for the Kick with Lorrin behind me. The next thing I hear is Lorrin telling me there is indeed a Black Bear a few feet behind us. I have no idea where that bear came from, maybe from under the walkway but there it was. I said that I would see Lorrin in the Kick and I was gone. No I did not run. Lorrin on the other hand went back to the walkway and took pictures.

Our luck with the weather had run short. It rained most of the time we were here, yet it certainly did not stop us from doing what we wanted to do. We spent many hours watching a few bears, both Black and Brown, as they waited for the salmon to make their way up the river. I think that the bears were as disappointed as we were that the salmon were late this season. No worries. The bears won't go hungry. There were a great many Chum Salmon out in the bay waiting for the right moment to make their run up the creek. They just weren't ready while we were there. Between sessions of watching the bears we did some touring as well. Fish Creek is about three miles passed Hyder and beyond that the road continues up into the Coast Mountains past glaciers and stunning vistas. Yes, it is foggy and rainy, not the best time to travel on dirt roads with steep slippery hills and twisting turns, still we take the chance to check it out and once again we were not disappointed. At the summit overlooking Salmon Glacier the clouds lifted enough to see this incredible icy glacier tumbling down the mountainside. A foggy day in the mountains is one of my favorite times, no kidding! This nether world is great for taking photographs, as mountains and valleys appear in the mist, foggy fingers clinging to ghostly trees and ridges one moment and then dissolved from sight the next. I was privileged to meet Keith Scott from New Brunswick, Canada while we were at the glacier overlook. He has studied and photographed bears since 1967; he has also published a number of books and DVD's about bears, very interesting and informative. I now have one of his books and a DVD; they both feature the Fish Creek Bears. The time we have spent here has been a great way to top off our 2008 adventure into the wild. I found it hard to pull myself away, knowing that our travels would soon bring us back home and end this adventure.

We did find one more diversion on our way south through British Columbia, the less traveled, Sea to Sky Highway (#99) from Cache Creek to Vancouver. It is a narrow, winding, sometimes steep road with construction in full swing in preparation for the 2010 Winter Olympics at Whistler, BC. This was just what we needed to keep our minds off going home to all the unpacking and cleaning ahead of us. At this point, I would like to say that we got home without a hitch but that was not to happen! After 91 days on the road, on our last night out, we pulled into Nairn Falls Provincial Park and found a beautiful campsite, high on a bank, overlooking the Green River. It was a perfect evening, warm and quiet. The weather report had not called for anything out of the ordinary. We put out our awning and open all the windows to help keep us cool. Dinner was over and I had just come back from a short evening walk. Lorrin was still away when without warning, thunder rolled, lightening flashed, rain pelted down and a micro burst of wind hit the motor home. Inside it looked like a tornado, everything flying around. Outside, I could see tents being caught by campers as the tents lifted off trying to fly away. Before I could close the windows, the wind took aim at our awning, ripping the arms out of their brackets. In a blink of an eye everything came crashing down. Lorrin arrived in time to put the pieces back together the best he could. Luckily, while the bars were bent and broken we did get the awning rolled up and wired things together well enough to get us home. That was one adventure we could have done without! We had traveled more than 10,000 miles between the two vehicles, with nothing more than one broken hose clamp, a new starter for the Kick, 2 small chips in Rika's windshield and one punctured tire on the Kick, a small finishing nail, easily repaired. Now a new awning is in our future!

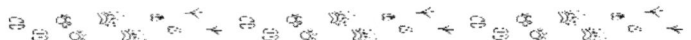

Black Bear *[19] [BC, YT, AK],* **Brown Bear** *[21] [AK],* **Polar Bear** *[#0] oh yes, my favorite woodland creatures! They behaved everywhere we went. As much as I am frightened of them, I did seek them out and I was delighted to see them, even with my heart jammed firmly in my throat. Black Bears are everywhere and seem to like showing up for my viewing pleasure (?). However, it was the Brown Bears I was really looking for. We did get to see quite a few. Now you may ask what about Grizzly Bears, well we are told that Brown Bears and Grizzly Bears are one in the same genetically speaking. It is the food they eat that makes the difference. The Browns diet is largely fish and they grow larger because of their rich diet. Grizzlies live inland and their diet is made up mostly of roots, berries, ground squirrels and such, they are smaller. Well, I guess, size is relative. I think they are all big enough. To set the record straight, I had no hopes of seeing a Polar Bear, as they are very*

rarely seen during the summer, in the areas that we traveled. Although in the summer of 2007 there was one in the Prudhoe Bay area that caused quite a fuss. I guess I will just have to go back and try again real soon!

In the years ahead, you will be more disappointed by the things that you let pass you by, then in the things that you have taken the time to experience! So pack up your rig, lock up the house and set your GPS for Adventure, up North!

Explore   Dream   Discover

Signpost Forest, Watson Lake, BC

Lorrin putting up our sign
At Watson Lake, BC

We only had to use the bug nets
a few times.

Trying to decide if he really had too!

Having a laugh!

HINTS FOR TRAVEL
HINTS IN THE LAST FRONTIER (NYLA)

I have repeated some of the hints from the "Adventures" here. It may seem redundant but I find these worth revisiting.

<u>Animal Safety</u> = If you stop to take a photo, make sure you are off the road and safe. Parking your rig in the middle of the road is not wise! Remember the shoulder may be soft and you may find yourself stuck in the mud! Not good! Don't get out of your rig if wildlife is nearby. Remember out of your rig and onto their dinner plate! Do not honk at a bull moose as he may think you are challenging him for his mate! That could be a big problem, unless you like dents in your rig. If you go hiking make noise as you walk. The last thing you want to do is surprise a Grizzly Bear or cow Moose and calf! The number one thing to remember is, animals are not tame and they are unpredictable! Parks, Visitor Information Centers and Ranger Stations have great information for keeping you safe and keeping the wildlife happy, make sure you get the information and FOLLOW IT! If you what to increase your chances of seeing wildlife, watch for other rigs parked on the side of the road and check it out. If they are all pointing their cameras in the same direction, more than likely there is something interesting to see.

<u>Binoculars and or a High Power Spotting Scope</u> = you will have a better chance of seeing and enjoying the animals with these.

<u>Border Crossing</u> = There are many regulations when crossing border into Canada and back into the U. S. They are always updating them. I will not go into the details here. Remember that you should be aware of what paperwork you need for each person in your vehicle; your pets; guns; vehicle insurance etc.

Checkout the official websites for Canada and the U. S. for the current information.

Bug Netting and Electric Fly Swatter = the netting to cover our heads came in handy two times on our trip. It would seem almost unnecessary to bother with them but if the bugs are thick you will bless your for-thought for having them! We bought the electric Fly swatter for a joke and found it really did work to get those pesky critters.

Camera and Computer = you will be disappointed if you don't have them! If you are a tecno geek, bring your computer and transfer those photos each day to keep up and keep track. There is nothing so sad as to lose track of where and when you took that *"Once in a life time"* photo! Besides if you take a few minutes every day, your photo journal will be ready for a final edit when you get home. Always document as you go! Your computer will come in handy to keep in touch with family and friends back home as many of the RV camps have Wi-Fi in this day and age.

Car and Health Insurance = Make sure you are covered for out of country and on the back roads, for both you and your rigs. We got travel insurance for us in case one of us had a major illness and needed to be medi-vaced home.

Cell Phones = Expect, NOT, to be able to use them unless you are near a town or city.

Dress in Layers = Do not take only heavy clothing. Pack cloths that you can layer as it gets colder or warmer. As you travel you will continually go through what I call climate changes from morning to evening. You will find the temperature changing and the weather fluctuating from rainy to sunny. It is easier to add a layer or remove a layer instead of changing cloths all the time.

Fishing, Clamming and Hunting = Check for regulations before you do anything. They are easy to get and you will not have to look over your shoulder for those Fish and Game folks!

Park Passes = Get your National Park pass and any other that you can. They will save you money.

Pharmacy = Insect repellent, sunscreen, first-aid-kit and any prescription drugs you may need. Speaking of prescriptions, have your doctor "write" out any prescriptions you are taking. If you have to have one filled while you are on your vacation, it will make getting it much easier. This is very important, even if you have enough to last for your trip, things happen and you could be without your medicines. It is much easier to hand the pharmacist a prescription then to call your doctor, have the prescription sent to a pharmacist where you are. This can take several days or even more if it happens to be a weekend! Having a short medical history and of course your doctors and pharmacists phone numbers and address could help in an emergency.

Remote Areas = If you plan on traveling for long times in remote areas, leave your information, times, dates in and out, etc with a friend or relative and remember when you come back out, let them know you are out! Always have a first-aid kit, extra food, water and warm clothes for emergencies. And make sure you have enough fuel.

$$$$ = Things cost more. Try to have a fair supply of staples and money! There isn't a grocery store on every corner. For that matter, there aren't very many corners and the gas stations are far and few between! Plan ahead!

The Weather Map Myth

Where is Alaska "really" located?

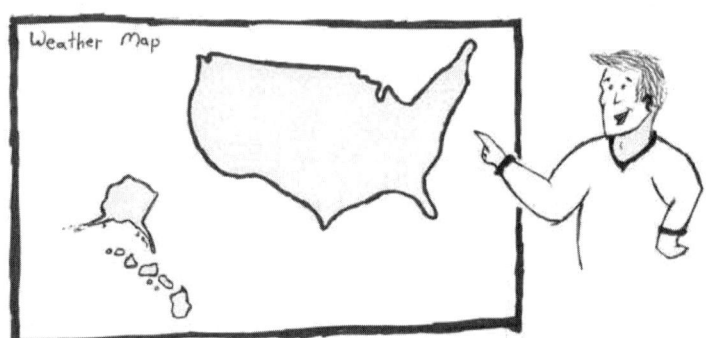

No wonder we get confused! Our friendly and very helpful weatherman doesn't seem to know where Alaska is. I have been told by travelers that "You can't possibly drive to Alaska, because it is an island out in the Pacific Ocean, near Hawaii!"

Thanks for the warning!

HINTS FOR TRAVEL & SAFETY (LORRIN)

The more you put into planning your trip to Alaska, the more enjoyable your trip will be. I am not talking about planning your trip hour by hour, just the overall basics. One of the first things you need to understand about Alaska is its size. When we were on the road promoting cruises and cruise tours to Alaska and Yukon Territory, one of the analogies we used was a road atlas. It is something that everyone is use to using. Have you ever noticed that every state fits a page? And some of the big states even get 2 pages? The one we used as an example gave Alaska 1/2 page! Alaska is 1/5th the size of the lower 48 states and has more coastline than all 3 coasts combined. You will find that distances between points will be further and take longer than you might think.

First you must decide on what you want to see and what modes of transportation you will take during your trip. For many folks a cruise on one of the many luxury cruise ships that leave from Seattle or Vancouver is their first introduction to what is waiting for them up north. Cursing to Alaska is the most scenic cruising in the world, but you will only see 1% of Alaska and none of the Yukon if that is all you do. Cruising coupled with an organized land tour is a good way to experience the Great Land without the concerns of going it on your own. It gives you a taste, without the worry.

There are many other ways to travel, such as, fly to Anchorage or Fairbanks and rent a RV for your adventure. Some folks will cruise one way rent a RV for a week or two and then fly the other way. If you have your own RV you could choose to drive both directions, take the Alaska State Ferry one way and drive the other, or ship your rig via Totem Ocean Trailer Express, known as TOAT, and fly or cruise to or from. If you decide to ship your rig via TOAT you would need to deliver it to Tacoma, Washington or Anchorage, Alaska. There are also organized caravans that will do all the planning for you, such as your itinerary including all your campsites, some entertainment, and there is a Wagon Master to keep everything going well and provide information to make your trip more interesting. By the end of the trip you will have made lots of new friends too. We talked to several people that bought a smaller rig just for their trip to Alaska, to save ware and tear on their primary RV.

Being that Nyla and I have both worked cruise ships and cruised to Alaska many times we wanted to concentrate on the land portion of the north. The organized cruise tours and land tours can give a good over view, and an excellent way to visit the Great Lands for the first timers, giving you a better understanding of what you will want to go back to see on your own. For us, there were those special places that we would like to stop at and stay forever, figuratively speaking. When I planned our trip, I laid it out in one-week sections of about 600-800 miles. That would allow us to travel an average of 150 miles a day and have 2 extra days to use as we wished. I did not want to have any fixed time schedules to meet, but as our plans progressed, a few did creep in. *[1.] our son flew in to meet us in Anchorage for a few weeks of fishing [2.] we made reservations in Denali National Park to ensure that we would get to camp in the interior of the park and [3.] our overnight hotel stay in Deadhorse.* Sometimes we did not use the extra days, but there were times when we got some place that was just too nice and we stayed longer, because we did not have a, too tight schedule.

A word to the driver! Remember if you slow down and follow the rules of driving on adverse roads, your rigs will come back in good shape. The stories you hear of rigs being shaken to pieces on the roads up north don't have to be the norm, if only you will pay attention to the conditions!

HINTS FOR TRIP PREPARATION (LORRIN)

There are a lot of things to consider when planning any trip and especially when going to Alaska and Yukon Territory. If you have never traveled in Alaska it is difficult to grasp the vastness of the Great Land. Like when the sign says "No Services for the next 250 miles." It doesn't mean there are no service stations, it means that you may not see any evidence that people exist, except for the road you are driving on. You need to be self-sufficient. Evan more than normal for an RV!

I took a basic set of tools and miscellaneous things like hose clamps, tie wraps, baling wire, electric and hand tire pumps, and of course, the fix it all, duct tape. I also took spare light bulbs, air filters, and such. For our tow vehicle, I even took a second spare tire, which is highly recommended when going to places like Prudhoe Bay. During our earlier travels I had noticed where rocks had been hitting the oil cooler that hangs down below the radiator on our motorhome. I built a guard and covered it with hardware cloth to protect it and I also covered the grill with heavy duty plastic screening. Something that I saw many people do was to put clear adhesive sheets, like shelf paper, on the front of the vehicle for protection against small rocks and bug splats. When we go again, I will probable do that too. Check your exhaust system, ours had over 3 feet at the end that was unsupported. The vibration of the roads could cause a problem with that much overhang. I put a rubber type exhaust hanger near the tip, which allowed it to move a little, but did not allow it to put undue stress on the rest of the system.

Protecting your tow vehicle is a different issue. There is no one-way to do it as every rig is different and has its own needs. What I did and how it worked for us, could be totally wrong for you application.

I made covers for the headlights from impact resistant plastic and attached them with nylon locking adhesive fasteners.

I installed a "bra", which covered the front and the hood. The hood portion turned out to not work as well as I had hoped. The airflow from the back of the motorhome lifted it and started to rub the paint on the hood.

We also made a cover for the windshield, to keep the rocks from hitting it.

I installed a full width flap across the back of the motorhome and still got rocks on our tow, even on to the roof. I plan on putting a second set of flaps behind the rear wheels of the motorhome in the future and we will make a full cover that will cover the Kick from hood to the roof.

I did not install a CB radio in our motorhome before we left and wished I had. The public service radios are handy to have for communication between rigs, but are of little use on the back roads where the ability to communicate with the big rigs would have been very helpful. Next time, I will also take a portable CB unit for our tow vehicle.

HINTS TO STRETCH YOUR TRAVEL $$$$ (LORRIN)

Even with the price of everything increasing there are things you can do to keep costs down.

We like to do a lot of boondocking and stays in government parks, which can cost as little as nothing. This trip, we stayed in a RV park with all the amenities about once a week, so we could do laundry, replenish water, empty our holding tanks, email, and whatever else we needed to do. This can take your nightly cost from the $30 range to an average of about $10. Over 3 months that saved us about $1800.00. There are also various camping clubs and organizations that you may have membership in, getting you great discounts along the way.

Fuel is another large cost for the trip. There are many things that you can do to reduce your fuel consumption. Start by inventorying your rigs, (motorhome, tow, trailer, etc.) and remove anything that you don't need. Next weigh the rigs and readjust the load, as necessary, for good balance. Check all your tires for proper inflation for the loading of your rigs.

The cost of fuel is always a hot topic when discussing a trip to the Great North. Most people will tell you that the cheapest prices will be in the major towns. Well in some cases that was true, but we also found that sometimes the station out in the middle of nowhere was cheaper than some stations in town. Even in the same little town we found a price spread of over $0.30 a gal. It generally will be more expensive in the tourist areas, but just because a station is a long way from anywhere, it may be on the delivery route and it costs less to deliver fuel to them that the next town.

Dump your holding tank whenever possible and evaluate where you will be going between now and the next chance of re-supplying. There are times you will need to have full water and fuel tanks, but there are other times that half will do, and this reduces the weight that you are packing around.

I know it sounds Un-American, but slow down. Even 5 mph will make a big difference in how much fuel you use.

We also used our tow a lot. We put over 4,000 miles on it alone. We planned our locations to camp so we could hub and spoke on day trips. 30 mpg verses 7 mpg let me think about that, not for very long though.

Keep things clean. On the dirt roads they use calcium carbonate to control dust and surface conditions. It is a corrosive that needs to be cleaned off within a reasonable time but it can also build up large amounts of dirt under your rigs, which adds weight.

Traffic on the Taylor Hwy

Road conditions can be good or bad on the Taylor Hwy

ADVENTURES IN COOKING ON THE ROAD

When we are traveling in our motor home, we rarely eat out and often eat simply, cheese and crackers for lunch, fresh homemade soup for dinner. Every so often though I get the itch to do something a bit more exciting or maybe we find some juicy local tidbit along the way that inspires me to do something a little different.

More often than not I have leftovers to do something with, make soup or a casserole. You know, that need to clear out the refrigerator.

As you travel you may want to try some of the local treats; seafood; fruit; Reindeer; Bison; and how about rhubarb or cabbage. The produce in Alaska is wonderful! The growing season is short, but the daylight is long and everything shoots up out of the ground in great profusion. The cabbage is as big as a house, well, OK, maybe a small house! It is always fun to catch a fish, pick some wild berries and check out what's fresh at the local farmers market, for something different, to spice up your dinning. Speaking of spice, I found some really great locally produced blends of spices and mustards, at the Farmers Market in Fairbanks.

I started a sourdough starter pot in honor of all the "sourdoughs" from the past. It was great fun trying out different recipes. There is nothing like the smell of fresh baked bread wafting through a campsite to whet your appetite, yum.

Because space in a RV is at a premium, in the cupboards, freezer and refrigerator, I have come up with a few tips to save space and weight.

I stock my cupboards and refrigerator for a long sashay in the wilderness with staples like pickles; olives; dry onion chips; crushed garlic; noodles; instant rice; potatoes; bagged rice mixes; flour; corn meal; cooking oil; sugar; evaporated milk; instant pudding; spices nuts; block cheeses of several kinds including shredded and Velveeta cheese; bacon bites; summer sausage; beef sticks and several different kinds of crackers. Canned meats – beef; ham; turkey; chicken; tuna; Spam; corned beef; deviled ham are great. With this kind of stock on hand I do not have to hit the grocery stores often, more time for fun on the road! You will want to customize this list to your tastes and needs.

A word of caution about food produces when you are going into Canada. There are some restrictions on meat, alcohol and other foods. www.canadawelcomesyou.net this website is a good place to get current information.

I start buying shelve-stable foods several months ahead of our trip departure date while I am doing my normal weekly shopping. This saves time and I can take advantage of specials and sale prices. I find making a general list of goods that I have and what I still need to buy, keeps me from over buying or for that matter forgetting something I need.

UHT Milk - If you don't know about this is product, I suggest you check it out. It is boxed milk that does not need to be refrigerated until it is opened. It comes in 8 ounce and 1 quart sizes and whole or 2%. I had a hard time finding it in grocery stores around my home, but most every grocery store in Alaska has it. There are times when you can't get to a store and it is nice to have a few of these tucked away for the day you run short.

🪶 Don't get me wrong, I like to check out grocery stores up north as they have some handy items that you might like to try. Often folks living up north do not have electricity and need things that do not need to be refrigerated. You might find something that you can use. In Watson Lake I came across a boxed desert that I could not resist. It was a "Robin Hood" brand, Nanaimo Bar mix. Very yummy and easy to boot!

🪶 I bought red flexible silicone bake-ware for the galley. What I had been using were old castoffs from our sailboat. They were a bit "rusty" from the salt air. I used this as a good excuse to buy a new bread pan, a square cake pan, a splatter lid and a muffin pan. They are less weight and there is no clattering while going down the road. Food does not stick in them and they will never rust. This was a great investment for the motor home. They really made my time in the galley easier.

🪶 **Vacu-pack** – Food products that can be sealed into vacuum bags will last longer in the freezer or on the shelf if vacuum sealed. I remove the excess packaging and divide into usable portions. Bulk Bacon Bits (I use the real bacon that you can get in large bags at warehouse stores). They can be vacu-packed in smaller portions (I put about ½ cup portions in each bag, to be used in scrambled eggs etc). By using bacon that is already fried you eliminate cooking messy, greasy bacon and you only have to deal with small amounts at a time.

🪶 **Dried Vegetables** - Such as frozen peas, peas/carrots mix, whole kernel corn. I have not tried others as these give me a good variety. I buy 2 pound bags of frozen vegetables. It is easy and quick. Dry them in a food dryer, according to the dryer instructions. Put them on the shelf in airtight containers. Rehydrate as needed along the way. ½ cup dried vegetables equates to about 1 ½ cups rehydrated. This saves room in your freezer and takes up little room on your shelve.

Frozen Fresh Vegetables - I chopped fresh onion, green and red peppers divided them into small portions and put them in small freezer bags and stored them in the freezer. *They could be put up in vacu-pack bags if you prefer,* to be used later in casseroles, soups etc. A nice side benefit when we crossed the border into Canada, I did not have to give up my fresh veggies. There is less spoilage; more room in your refrigerator and fewer stops to buy fresh groceries. I try to get them when they are on sale to help cut costs.

Wild Treats - Fireweed jelly, berries, wild-meats, fresh vegetables are some of the wild treats that you can try while you are on the road in Alaska.

This is my disclaimer, right up front! I am not a cordon bleu chef. I almost never measure anything or use the exact same ingredients each time. Try these recipes (*at your own risk*) and remember to be flexible using what you have on hand. None of the recipes are complicated, so have fun and get started.

BREADS & SOURDOUGH GOODIES

Garlic Cheese Biscuits

2 cups biscuit mix

2/3 cup milk

½ cup shredded sharp cheddar cheese

¼ cup butter, melted

¼ teaspoon garlic powder

Place in bowl to mix: Biscuit mix; Milk; Cheese

Mix until soft dough forms (do not over mix)

Drop dough by spoonfuls onto ungreased cookie sheet

Bake 8-10 minutes at 450 degrees F until golden brown

Mix butter and garlic power brush over warm biscuits

Serve warm

Makes about 10 biscuits

Spoon Bread

3/4 cup cornmeal, stone or water ground is the best

1 teaspoon salt

1 cup boiling water

3 tablespoons melted butter

2 large eggs

1 cup milk

2 teaspoons baking power

Combine cornmeal and salt in a mixing bowl, stirring constantly. Slowly add boiling water and then melted butter. Beat eggs in separate bowl until light yellow and add milk and beat to mix. Add milk/egg mix to cornmeal mixture and then baking power. Wisk to blend, turn in to a well greased 8" square pan. Bake at 350 degrees for 30 minutes, until firm.

Serve with lots of butter I like sour cream on it too. I sometimes toss into the batter ½ cup frozen corn kernels or a handful of shredded cheddar cheese or bacon bits or 1 cup creamed corn they are all good - cilantro or chives would work too.

Sourdough Starter

You can buy a starter pack just about anywhere up north and follow their directions. They come with recipes to try out.

Or try this one for a quick start.

2 cups filtered water

1½ teaspoons dry yeast

2 cups all purpose flour

3 tablespoons sugar

Mix all ingredients in a glass bowl until smooth *(never use metal spoons or bowls when working with your starter, as it may react poorly)*. Cover with a clean dishtowel and leave in a warm spot, stirring once a day and remove 1 cup of starter every few days and replenish with ½ cup warm water and ½ cup flour every few days until bubbles appear on the surface. It takes longer sometimes then others to get started. When it has started to bubble you can refrigerate until needed. To keep it active it should be used every few weeks. Prior to using, bring to room temperature *(overnight is best)* each time you use the starter replace the amount you have removed with equal parts flour and water. For instance, if you have used 1 cup starter stir in ½ cup flour and ½ cup water. Let the starter stand at room temperature for 4 hours before you return it to the refrigerator. *Because I used my starter almost every day while we were traveling, I did not refrigerate it.*

To adapt most regular recipes, add 1 cup starter and use ½ cup less each flour and liquid.

128

For a more traditional starter
Boil 2 large russet potatoes *(with skin on)* until it falls apart. Remove skin, mash to a puree.

Cool add enough water to make 2cups rich potato water.

Add 2 tablespoons sugar

2 cups flour

Beat with a wooden spoon until it becomes a smooth creamy batter. Loosely cover with a clean cloth and set in a warm place to start fermentation. If you want to hurry it up add ½ teaspoon granulated yeast. In a glass bowl blend 2 cups warm potato water and 2 cups flour with a wooden or plastic spoon. Lightly cover with a clean cloth and place in a warm spot. Stir once a day. In 3-4 days bubbles should appear. *Using sugar will keep your sourdough a little sweeter.* Do not use too much sugar, as it will toughen up you bread. I use less sugar, as I like the sour smell and taste.

Remember every starter has its own personality, taste and needs. Some are very active bubbling almost immediately and others are slower. I suggest that you get acquainted with yours and if at first you don't succeed try, try again. It is great fun to come up with new ideas for your starter.

If you read all the cookbooks and information about sourdough starter, they say to put the starter in the refrigerator between uses. Because the miners used it most everyday they always kept the sourdough warm by tucking it into their shirt when it was too cold. They didn't want it to freeze. Now I am not going that far but I have chosen not to put my starter in the refrigerator. I kept mine in a glass container on the counter or in the sink if we are under way. I used it every few days to keep it active and healthy stirring it several times a day. I find talking to it helps too!

(Remember always replenish your starter after you use it)

When making bread *and you are trying to keep your bread dough warm while it is raising and the temperature in your RV is a little cool, try heating up some water in your microwave and then put the dough in the microwave with the hot water to keep the dough warm. Do not start the microwave while the dough is rising.*

Sourdough Flapjacks

2 cups milk
2 cups flour
1 egg
2 tablespoons sugar
½ teaspoon soda
½ teaspoon salt
1 cup sourdough starter
Mix all ingredients and fry up as you would regular pancakes. Serve with your homemade Fireweed syrup!

Sourdough Biscuits

2 cups flour
1 teaspoon salt
½ teaspoon baking soda
1 teaspoon baking powder
½ cup soft butter or a little more than ¼ cup vegetable oil
1 cup sourdough starter
½ cup milk, room temperature
Combine flour, soda, salt and baking powder, cut in butter until coarse mixture. Next, with a fork mix in milk and starter to form

a soft dough. Turn onto a floured board and softly knead. Pat out until it is a ½ thick, cut with a 3 inch cutter or just cut into squares. Place on cookie sheet and loosely cover with plastic wrap. Set aside for 30 minutes. Bake at 425 degrees F for 12 minutes or until golden brown. Serve with honey and butter. Eat them hot out of the oven. Just don't burn your tongue!

Sourdough Cranberry Pineapple Pecan Muffins

½ cup dried cranberries and 8 ounce canned, crushed pineapple including juice, *add water if needed to cover fruit,* bring to a boil and set aside to soften and cool.

1 cup starter

1 cup vegetable oil

½ cup milk, room temperature

2 eggs

1 cup sugar

½ cup chopped pecans

1½ cup flour

1 teaspoon vanilla extract

2 teaspoons baking powder

½ teaspoon salt

Drain the cranberries and pineapple, *make sure that the fruit is cooled to room temperature,* add all liquids, mix together and then add the dry ingredients mix. Pour into muffin pan. Filling each 2/3 full and bake at 350 degrees F for 25 minutes. I had too much batter for the muffin tin I have so baked the rest in a cake pan and served as dessert. I baked the cake about 40 minutes.

Lemon Friendship Cake

1 cup sourdough starter
1 cup vegetable oil
½ cup milk
3 eggs
2 cups sugar
1 teaspoon lemon extract
2 cups flour
1 ½ teaspoon baking powder
½ teaspoon baking soda
½ teaspoon salt
1 small box lemon instant pudding mix or other flavor if you like
2 tablespoons poppy seeds
Topping:
1/3 cup sugar
½ teaspoon lemon flavoring
If you use a different a pudding flavor change the topping flavor and use chopped nuts and raisins instead of poppy seeds.

In a large bowl, combine the starter, oil, milk, eggs, sugar and lemon flavoring, mix well. Add dry ingredients on top of moist mixture flour *(baking powder, baking soda, salt and pudding mix)* stir to combine add poppy seeds stir some more. Grease two 9" x 5" x 3" loaf pans and pour into pans. Sprinkle with lemon sugar to lightly cover top.

Bake at 325 degrees F for one hour or until a toothpick comes out clean. Remove from pans and cool on a rack.

Sourdough Beignets

These rectangular "doughnuts" are a New Orleans icon. If you want to make beignets for breakfast, the dough can be refrigerated overnight then rolled out, cut and fried the next morning.

1 teaspoon yeast
½ cup warm water
¼ cup sugar
1 cup sourdough starter
½ teaspoon salt
1 egg
2 tablespoons vegetable oil
½ cup evaporated milk
2 ½ to 3 ½ cups flour
Light oil for deep frying* *(see note)*
Powdered sugar for dusting

In mixing bowl, sprinkle yeast over warm water, stir in 2 teaspoons of the sugar until dissolved. Set aside for about 10 minutes, until small bubbles begin to form. Add the remaining sugar, starter, salt, egg, oil and evaporated milk and mix well. Stir in 1½ cups of the flour and beat until smooth. Add the remaining flour a little at a time until the dough pulls away from the sides of the bowl and becomes too stiff to stir with a spoon. Turn the dough out onto a floured board. Form into a ball and transfer to a clean, lightly greased bowl, turning to coat all sides. Cover with plastic wrap and let rise in warm place for 1½ to 2 hours. *Or if desired cover and refrigerate overnight, then the next day, proceed as follows.*

Roll dough to a thickness between 1/8" and ¼", cut into rectangles about 2" by 3". Heat oil in a large deep pot to a depth of 3" to 4" to 360 degrees F (I did them in a small pot one at a time, you have to watch the temperature more closely as it will fluctuate more because of its small volume). Fry 3 or 4 at a time, until they puff and become golden on both sides, about 2 to 3 minutes, turning once or twice. Drain on racks set over paper towels. Sprinkle heavily with powdered sugar and serve immediately. Makes about 3 dozen yummy bites of heaven!

*NOTE: In New Orleans, beignets are fried in cottonseed oil, but you can use any light-colored, mild-tasting oil, such as canola.

The author of this recipe has graciously given me permission to print it from the book I bought while in Skagway. **(Simply Sourdough -- The Alaska Way by Kathy Doogan, Todd Communications, 611 E. 12th Street, Anchorage, Alaska, 99501-4603,** sales@Toddcom.com**)** I have enjoyed trying many of the recipes and every one of them turned out to be delectable! Kathy tells me that she and her husband favor the raisin bread and cornmeal millet bread.

For tasty sourdough dumplings see "Main Dishes" section.

CAKE and PIE

Wild Berry Coffee Cake

1 ½ cup all purpose floor
¾ cup white sugar
2 ½ cups baking powder
1 teaspoon salt
¼ cup vegetable oil
¾ cup milk
1 egg
1 ½ cup wild berries mix and match

1/3 cup all purpose flour
½ cup brown sugar, packed
½ teaspoons cinnamon
¼ cup firm butter
Blend thoroughly, 1 ½ cups flour, sugar, baking powder, salt, oil, egg, milk
Stir in berries
Pour into greased 9" cake pan
Combine 1/3 cup flour, brown sugar, cinnamon and butter
Sprinkle over batter and top with remaining berries
Bake at 375 degrees F for 25-30, minutes or until done.
Serve warm with butter and honey

Strawberry Rhubarb Pie
Pie dough for a double pie crust
3 cups chopped raw rhubarb
1 cup fresh strawberries sliced
1 ½ cup white sugar
3 tablespoons minute tapioca
¼ teaspoon salt
½ teaspoon nutmeg
2 tablespoons butter
Mix rhubarb, berries, tapioca, salt, and nutmeg in a bowl and let stand for ½ hour. Turn into 9" pie shell and dot with butter, cover with lattice top pastry. Bake in preheated 400 degrees F for 10 minutes. Reduce heat to 350 degrees F and bake 35 minutes longer, until crust is golden and fruit is cooked through.
Serve warm with French Vanilla ice cream.

Tartar Sauce for Fish

I don't always have store bought tartar sauce when I want to do a fish meal. No worries, I make some. It is never the same twice and always depends on what I have on the shelf, what I am doing to the fish and what kind of fish I am cooking.

1 cup mayonnaise

¼ cup finely chopped pickles *(sweet or dill, your taste counts)*

2 tablespoons finely chopped sweet onion

1 teaspoon crushed garlic

1 tablespoon lemon or lime juice

Dash white pepper to taste

½ teaspoon green Tabasco sauce

Mix all together and refrigerate for at least 1 hour to let the flavors blend.

Salmon – Baked or Grilled

I am a minimalist when it comes seasoning fish, especially with salmon. I am also very particular that fish must be fresh, water to pan! The older the fish the more seasoning is my rule.

Having said that here is what I do with a nice fillet. For a fillet I figure about 8 ounces per person depending on how hungry they are.

Baked:

Place the fillet skin side down on a large square of heavy foil and then do one of the following.

[1.] For a 2 pound fillet - mix ½ cup brown sugar, 2 tablespoons melted butter with enough lemon or orange juice to make a thick paste. Smear the paste on the flesh/top side. Seal the foil and bake at 350 degrees for ½ hour or until fillet is cooked through. It should be flaky.

[2.] Cover fillet with sliced sweet onion, lemon or orange slices and drizzle with melted butter. Seal foil and bake.

[3.] Try one of the seafood seasoning on the market today. Rub it over the flesh side seal and bake. Any of these can be done on a grill as well. Put the foil package on indirect heat of the grill. I would double wrap with foil for this.

[4.] I have recently found, at the grocery store a foil, smoker bag to use in the oven, on the grill or even over a campfire. It has some alder chips in an inner pocket and you slide the fillet in and bake according to directions, it comes with some good recipes. Give it a try, I liked it.

[5.] Crab & Shrimp, Stuffed Salmon - If you have a whole salmon or a large roast cut King, about 6 pounds, clean, scale, cut the head and tail off. In a large bowl mix ½ pound cooked crabmeat, ½ pound small pieces raw shrimp, ½ cup melted butter, 1 tablespoon chopped parsley, ¾ cup chicken broth, ½ cup fine chopped onion, ½ cup fine celery, 1 to 1 ½ cup fresh bread crumbs, salt and pepper to taste. Stuff and tie with cooking twine to hold stuffing in, place in a shallow roasting pan. Cover lightly with foil and bake at 350 degrees F. To determine cooking time, measure the thickness of the fish at its thickest point and allow 10 minutes per measured inch. This should be enough to serve about 8 hungry friends.

Grilled:

[1.] Cedar planked: Buy a cedar plank for cooking and follow the directions that come with it and grill. If you want more smoke flavor, make a foil lid to set over the fish, to keep the smoke closer.

[2.] Drunken Salmon: 1 large salmon fillet (skin on), spicy mustard (Dijon), 1/3 cup butter, 1 cup brown sugar, ½ cup dark rum, salt and pepper to taste. Lay foil over rack spray no stick grill oil on foil. Salt and pepper fillet and cover with a thin coating of mustard. Place fillet skin-side up on foil on hot grill. Cook for about 5 minutes. Turn fillet over and spread with a thick paste of mustard, butter, brown sugar and rum. Cook until salmon is flaky, not dry, about 5 minutes more. [3.] A dry fish rub on salmon steaks and grilled works well too.

Smoked Salmon Ball

8 ounces smoked salmon
16 ounces cream cheese softened
2 teaspoons lemon juice
3 tablespoons fresh chopped chives
1 tablespoon finely chopped sweet onion
  Mix together until completely blended and Serve on crackers.

Halibut Cakes

Other white fish may be used or why not try some crab
8 ounces Fresh halibut
½ cup white cooking wine
1 ½ cup fresh breadcrumbs
½ cup cooked wild rice
2 eggs beaten
¼ cup finely diced sweet onion
2 tablespoons red pepper
2 tablespoons green pepper
2 tablespoons mayonnaise
1 tablespoon Dijon mustard
1 tablespoon Worcestershire sauce

Dash lemon juice

½ cup clarified butter for frying

Bake skinned & boned fish and wine in baking dish at 400 degrees F until it is flaky, *about 10 minutes.* Remove the fish from the wine and crumble into a large bowl. Add half the breadcrumbs and the rest of the ingredients, *reserving the butter.* Mix well. Scoop ½ cup portions packed tightly. Place on wax paper and form into patties. Cover both sides with the rest of the breadcrumbs

Refrigerate for 2 -3 hours *(At this point they may be sealed and frozen for later frying)* Melt butter into a large non-stick skillet, med-high, fry till golden brown on both sides. Serve with lemon and tartar sauce.

This makes 4 large cakes. Before we leave on a long trip I will make a double batch of this recipe and freeze them individually for a quick savory meal on the road.

Steamed Clams

2 pounds small fresh steaming clams in shell

1 bottle white wine *(the cheap kind)*

¼ cup fresh parsley finely chopped

2 tablespoons chopped chivies

1 tablespoon chopped fresh garlic

If you dig the clams yourself rinse them and let set in fresh water for a few hours before you cook them. Refresh the water if it gets cloudy. *This will give them time to spit out any sand.* Scrub clams and check that none are filled with mud, *yuck*! Place all ingredients in a deep soup pot and cook over moderate heat until clams open. Do not drain, the juice is good for dipping your bread into. Serve with crusty garlic sourdough bread and butter. This can be the whole meal! Nothing more is needed.

Clam Chowder

4 ounces beacon chopped into small chunks
1 clove garlic crushed
½ cup chopped sweet onion
4 cups cream
½ cup flour
1 cup clam broth *(chicken broth can used instead)*
¾ cup thinly diced celery
1 teaspoon parsley finely chopped
10 ounces clams fresh-cooked or canned
6 medium red potatoes, cooked and cubed skin on
Salt & Pepper to taste
Tobacco sauce
Chives

Wash and scrub potatoes and boil then cube, set aside. In soup pot fry bacon, garlic and onion until the onion is soft. Next blend cream, flour and broth adding it to the pot. Add celery and parsley then heat over medium heat until thickened *(do not let it scorch)*. Add clams and potatoes then simmer over low heat for up to an hour. Season to your taste with salt; pepper; Tabasco sauce and garnish with fresh chives. *If you don't have fresh potatoes, try a box of scalloped potatoes and a little more broth, cooking until potatoes are soft.* Serve with fresh, hot sourdough bread.

MAIN DISHES & SOUPS

Meats for Main Dishes

While we are on long trips I always try to have a variety of canned meats on the shelf for main dishes, ham, turkey, chicken, tuna, spam, hash, roast beef or corned beef. I take a can *(12 ounce)* of meat and pair it with rice, mashed potatoes, noodles etc. By changing the ingredients around, the main dish will take on a different taste for never a dull dinner. Let's see, Chinese, German, Mexican, you can go around the world with this idea. Let your imagination take a walk on the wild-side! Give these ideas a try:

Beefed up Chili

½ cup chopped onion
½ cup red/green sweet pepper, mix or match
Sauté veggies in pot until are soft
Add 1 can chili with beans, size depends on how many are hungry folks you are serving
1 can *(12 ounce)* beef *(chicken)*
Add spices to your taste. I like to add Green Pepper Tabasco sauce to give it an extra kick.
Simmer until flavors blend. Serve topped with shredded cheese and sour cream with crusty bread on the side. Or how about spoon bread instead. I use a spoon bread mix or you can do it from scratch. Served over rice is good too.

141

Chicken and Dumplings

Quick and tasty for a rainy day, cook up something hearty. The aroma will comfort you and it will taste good too!

1 can *(12 ounce)* chicken drained

1 cup peas, carrots, corn mixed or any combination there of

1 can cream of chicken soup

1 tablespoon onion flakes

1/2 cup green/red sweet pepper chopped total

½ cup milk

Combine above ingredients in a large pot and heat. While chicken is heating up, mix up dumpling as follows.

1½ cup flour

½ teaspoon baking soda

1 teaspoon salt

1 teaspoon baking powder

1/3 cup cooking oil

1 cup sourdough starter

½ cup milk

In a bowl combine flour, soda, salt and baking powder. Cut in oil with fork. Add sourdough starter, milk mix with fork to make a soft dough, *don't over mix*, this should be very light and fluffy. Spoon tablespoon sized lumps on top of hot chicken mixture. Cover with lid and turn heat down to simmer. Do not remove lid for about 10 minutes. Then take a quick peek. The dumplings should have plumped up and they should not look doughy.

This dumpling recipe is good with sauerkraut and brats too. Just fry up some brats in the pot and dump a can of sauerkraut on top of the brats and spoon dumping mixture on top. Simmer with lid on for about 10 minutes or until dumplings are done.

The number of brats and size of can of sauerkraut depends on how hungry you are.

Chicken Fried Rice

1 can *(12 ounce)* white meat chicken drained
1 tablespoon olive oil
½ cup chopped sweet onion
2 tablespoons green onion chopped
½ cup mixed red and green sweet pepper
2 eggs
3 cups cooked white rice
½ cup peas
½ teaspoon Green Pepper or Sweet & Spicy Tabasco Sauce
Fry sweet onion, peppers and canned chicken in oil. Scramble eggs into veggie mixture. Stir in rice and green onion and peas. Let simmer with lid on, for a few minutes, to let flavors combine.

Sheppard's Pie

1 can *(12 ounce)* roast beef
1 cup beef gravy *(an instant packet works well)*
½ cup sautéed onion
3 cups mashed potatoes
Spices to taste
Break up beef in the bottom of a casserole pan. Add onion and pour the gravy over the meat and onions. Spoon mashed potatoes over meat mixture and bake for ½ an hour. As everything in this recipe is already cooked it just needs to be hot though out. Serve with a dollop of sour cream.

Mexican Meat Sauce

Caned roast beef makes a good base for Mexican style meat sauce to use with nachos, tacos, burritos.

1 can *(12 ounce)* roast beef
1 can enchilada sauce
¼ cup chopped onions

Heat up ingredients in a sauce pan and use over nachos, in tacos or with burritos. Top with sour cream, shredded cheese, sliced black olives, fresh chopped tomatoes, hot peppers, green onion. I have been known to make up my own enchilada sauce with salsa or a bag of taco spice for seasoning.

Ham Quiche

Pie crust for one pie
1 can *(12 ounce)* ham drained
4 large eggs beaten
½ cup mayonnaise
1 cup milk
1 cup grated cheese, Monterey, cheddar, pepper-jack mix and match
½ cup chopped onion
½ cup sliced mushrooms
Salt and white pepper to your taste

Place uncooked crust in pie pan. In a bowl, whip eggs and mayonnaise. Mix in the rest of the ingredients and pour into piecrust. Bake at 425 degrees F for 15 minutes and reduce to 300 degrees and continue to bake for 30 minutes longer. Center should be just firming up. If you like serve with hollandaise sauce and grill brazed asparagus.

You can eliminate the ham and use instead 10 ounces fresh or canned crab meat.

Chicken/Bacon Rollup

One Chicken breast per person. Pound to flatten. Season with Mexican seasoning. Place on each breast Mexican shredded cheese chopped jalapeño peppers sautéed onion and any other vegetables to your taste. Fold over and wrap with a slice of bacon and hold with a toothpick. Grill until almost done. Last 10 minutes glace with teriyaki sauce. I was given this as an incomplete recipe, so I play with this one and change up the ingredients to suit my mood. Serve with rice.

Orange Honey Glazed Chicken

2 skinless chicken breasts
2 tablespoons honey
¼ cup orange juice
1 ¼ cup chicken broth
¼ cup chopped onion
½ cup instant white rice
2 tablespoons each parsley and chivies

Cook chicken and onion at med-high, in frying pan until browned. Coat chicken with juice and honey, continue to brown for just about 30 seconds. Remove chicken for now. Add broth and rice to the honey juice mixture, heat to boiling. Cover and cook over low heat for 10 minutes. Add chicken back into pan, cover and cook an additional 10 minutes. The last few minutes add parsley and chives. Serve with fresh vegetables.

Yukon Gold Potato Side Dish

4 tablespoons butter
10 ounces fresh mushrooms sliced *(if you know your mushrooms, wild are the best)*

2 tablespoons chives

1 ½ teaspoons salt

½ teaspoon ground white pepper

2 cups heavy whipping cream

Adding 1 cup shredded cheddar cheese is an option or a cup of cooked, crumbled and drained pork sausage to make it a main dish. Preheat oven 375 degrees F

Butter the baking dish, well. Melt butter in heavy skillet over medium heat. Add mushrooms, sauté until brown and soft. Wash and scrub potatoes, slice 1/8"thick. Layer mushrooms and potatoes, sprinkling each layer with a portion of the chives, salt and pepper. Top layer should be potatoes. Pour cream over casserole, cover with foil and bake for 45 minutes.

Uncover and continue to bake until golden brown and firm. *(15 - 20 minutes)*. Let stead for 5 minutes before serving.

Cream of Turkey Soup

(Chicken or ham would also work)

3 strips bacon cut into small strips

2 tablespoons butter

1 small onion chopped

2 tablespoons fresh chopped garlic

2 tablespoons each red pepper and green pepper

2 medium stalks celery diced small

2 tablespoons flour

3 cups chicken broth

1 – 15 oz. can cream of corn *(add 1 cup frozen corn if you like your soup corny)*

1 can *(12 ounce)* turkey *(chicken or ham)* small chucks

4 large Yukon Gold potatoes cut into small cubes

½ teaspoon thyme

¼ teaspoon white pepper
Salt to taste to your taste
2 cups milk *(cream canned or fresh if you like it thicker)*
¼ cup fresh cilantro finely chopped *(optional)*
(If you use ham in this recipe you might like some sharp cheddar cheese shredded over the soup after you ladle it into soup bowls). Fry the bacon and butter in a stockpot until crisp. Add in onion, celery, garlic, red pepper and green pepper, simmer until vegetables are tender. Add meat, potatoes, spices and stock and bring to a high simmer for 10 minutes. Combine flour and milk and add to pot. Continue to simmer until soup is thickened. Just before serving sprinkle cilantro over the soup.
All the fresh vegetables can be substituted for dried or frozen.
Serve with hot sourdough biscuits and butter or corn bread dripping with honey and butter.

Chicken Vegetable/Noodle Soup
This one is quick and easy. I like to make it as a light meal served with biscuits.
1 can (12 ounce) white chunk chicken
½ cup each chopped onions/green/red sweet peppers
8 cups water
2 cubes chicken bullion
Salt and pepper to taste
1 cup dry noodles
½ cup peas
½ cup carrots
½ cup corn
Salt and pepper to taste
Poultry seasoning to taste

Sauté onions and peppers in soup pot then add the rest of the ingredients bring to a boil and turn down to simmer. Simmer with lid on for about ½ hour or until flavors are blended and noodles are cooked. As always you can mix it up with what goes in the pot to your taste. Sometimes I like to put some Mexican seasons in to spice it up.

 **MISCELLANEOUS**

Fireweed Jelly

Good on toast, pancakes, and waffles

8 cups fireweed blossoms *(no green parts or stems)*

¼ cup lemon juice

4 ½ cups water

2 packages powdered pectin

5 cups sugar

Pick, wash and measure fireweed blossoms *(flower parts only)* ***Be sure that you find plants away from chemical spray).*** Add lemon juice and water to blossoms in a large pan. Boil for 10 minutes. Next strain the mixture and toss-out flower remnants. Heat strained juice until warm. Add pectin bring to a boil that you cannot stir down. Add sugar and again bring to a complete boil that you cannot stir down. Boil hard for 3 minutes. Pour into clean jars and seal. If for some reason this recipe does not jell completely, no worries, just call it "syrup" and pour it on your sourdough flapjacks!

Spam Spread

8 ounces soft cream cheese

4 ounces shredded cheddar cheese

1 can spam
1 tablespoon lemon juice
1 teaspoon Worcestershire sauce
2 tablespoons chives chopped
Mayonnaise and pepper to taste
Grate spam and cheddar cheese, mix with cream cheese and chives. Add juice and Worcester sauce. Mix with mayonnaise and pepper to taste. Spread on crackers or toast points.

Sandwich and Cracker Spreads
Those same canned meats that I use for main dishes can be used for sandwiches and cracker spreads. A can of meat plus mayo, mustard, relish, salt, pepper, crushed garlic, fine chopped sweet onion and shredded cheese to taste, makes a great spread for sandwiches, crackers, rolls, tortillas and such. By changing the ingredients around the spread will take on a different taste for never a dull lunch. Corned Beef with sauerkraut, Swiss cheese and Thousand Island dressing on rye bread, pan fried is a great treat with a dill pickle on the side.

Coleslaw
1 small cabbage, finely chopped
½ small purple onion, finely chopped
2 tablespoons cooked bacon crumbled
Dressing:
½ cup sugar
1 teaspoon salt
1 teaspoon dry mustard
1 teaspoon celery seed
1 cup white vinegar
 2/3 cup light vegetable oil

Combine cabbage, bacon and onion, set aside. Place dressing ingredients in a pot and bring to a boil. Pour hot over cabbage and toss. Refrigerate. This is great as a side salad or put a ½ cup on a hot corned beef on rye sandwich.

 ODE TO SOURDOUGH

What tasty, temping treats you make.
From Flapjacks to Beignets.
How versatile you can be.
I've had fun seeing what goodies you could deliver
Bread, cookies, cakes & more.
You bubbled and worked to make
The treats melt in the mouth yummy!
No longer do I stop at the bakery to buy.
I just reach for my treasured sourdough pot
It's oh so fragrant starter within.
Ready to do its self proud.
Bringing forth, delectable treats, for our tasting pleasure.
Thank you!
For making our adventure more delectable.
You are welcome to travel with us any time!

Spam is a staple in the frozen north. It does not freeze! If going snowmobiling Alaskans will tape a can of spam to the tail pipe of a snowmobile and by the time they get to their destination the spam will be hot and ready to eat. Did you know that Hawaii is the only state that eats more spam than Alaska?

GLOSSARY = Alaska Speak or How to Decipher what Alaskans are saying (Some May Be True)

Adventures (otherwise known as chapters) = are waiting for you in this book and up North, so let's get started!

Alaska Grown = a program that ensures quality in Alaskan agricultural production. This logo guarantees products have the finest flavor, freshness and appearance. Only products produced in Alaska are eligible for this certification of quality.

Alcan Highway = is the acronym for Alaska and Canada Highway. In more recent years the powers that be have opted to change the name to the Alaska Highway or Highway (YT #1, AK #2). Most likely because no one would go on the highway no matter how nice it was, after hearing the stories of broken windshields, flat tires and all the other hardships of the past. I still like to use Alcan when referring to the highway. So call me old fashion and stubborn, that is, who I am!

ATV = quad, 4 wheeler, all similar vehicles with big wheels used for travel off road through the bush.

Aurora Borealis = also known as Northern Lights are the natural light displays streaming across the winter sky of the far north. Mind you they can happen year round and any time of the day or night but you can only see them when it is dark and clear. There is a long scientific explanation for it. I'll just say that it has something to do with protons and electrons striking gas particles somewhere in the upper atmosphere and so much more. If you want to know more look it up on the internet, there is a ton of information waiting for you! What I will say is, once you have seen them dance across the sky you will never forget them!

Beluga Whale = or white whale is a small (11–16 feet) toothed whale that lives in the cold waters of the north.

Blue Tarps = you know those sheets of blue plastic that you can buy, in varying sizes, at the hardware store. You will see them everywhere. They are considered one of the two most important "building materials" in Alaska. No house is complete without at least one. They are also used to repair cars, boats, airplanes or anything else you might think of. (For the second most important see duct tape)

Boondocking = going out into the bush where there are no comforting amenities such as power and water but there will be solitude and wilderness.

Bore Tide = this event happens in just a few places in the world. You may have heard of the Bay of Fundy and how its water rushes in on some extreme tides. Alaska's Kink and Turnagain Arms have bore tides too. It occurs at the end of an extreme low tide. Maximum tides can be as much as 40 feet from high to low, when the water rushes back in to the arms (inlets). The water that is still trying to go out meets the water that is trying to come in. Where it meets the stronger incoming water rides up over the weaker out going water, creating a 2-6 foot wave that can move for miles up the arm at speeds of as much as 10 knots. This only happens once a day and only at extreme tides. Surfers like to try to catch these waves as it moves up the inlet but if they miss the wave, they will have a long wait for the next one.

Borough = Alaska is unique among the 50 states in that most of its land mass has not been organized into political subdivisions equivalent to the county form of government. Local government is by a system of organized boroughs, much like counties in other states. Some areas are not even included in any borough because of low population in those areas.

Braided River = This type of river is not deep, it is usually quite wide, with the water weaving its way back and forth crisscrossing around sandbars, creating the look from above, that someone has braided it.

Breakup = No, not when you send your partner packing after a long winter together in close quarters, otherwise known as cabin fever! This is a term used in the north to describe what happens to all that ice in the frozen rivers, after a long winter of snow and ice, the warmth of spring loosens winters grip on those frozen rivers, creating a spectacular show as the ice breaks loose, crumbling and rumbling its way down river. Some towns hold a lottery to guess when the exact time of breakup will occur on their river.

Bugs = Yep there are some up there!

Bush = no not the things that grow in the backyard. This is a term meaning "in the wilderness", where there are no roads. You may hear someone say, "I am going out into the bush". Translated, "I am going out into the wilderness", most likely to hunt, fish or live.

Bush Plane = this is a small airplane, often equipped with tundra wheels (big soft tires for landing on uneven terrain) snow skis (for winter) or pontoons (for lake and river landing) depending on where and when they plan on landing in the bush. The bush plane is used like their second car, along with ATVs and Snow Machines, as there are few roads out in the bush.

Cabin Fever = what can happen if winter is too long and dark and you don't get out and enjoy all that snow. The walls start to close in, you crave the sun and you go a little stir-crazy. A cure for cabin fever, long summer days. But don't wait for summer, winter can be the best time up north, when you can get out and explore. The ground, lakes and rivers are frozen, making it easier to get around with snowshoes, dog sleds, and snow machines. Some Alaskans are known to take a break from winter, say in nice hot, sunny Hawaii along about March. Guess they want to get acquainted with our 50th state.

Calaboose = jail

Cell Phone Service = intermittent at best!

Cheechako = Greenhorn, Newcomer, Newbee - Someone that has not spent a year or more in Alaska. The story goes, the term, Cheechako got its start way back when in the gold rush days a native asked a miner where he came from. The miner came from Chicago, but when it was repeated it did not come out sounding like Chicago, instead it sounded like Cheechako (chee-CHA-ko) and the name stuck. So if someone calls you a Cheechako don't be insulted, just stay longer.

Chinook Jargon = a combination of words from several languages, Native, English, French to form one language that all could converse in. This was a big help as travelers explored this vast land.

Combat Fishing = this is when you go fishing with 2 or 3 hundred of your closest buddies or at least, they will be by the end of the day. Sometimes, when the fish are running there will be literally hundreds of fisherman standing shoulder to shoulder all hoping that they catch the big one. Most of the time they play nice!

Duct Tape = sometimes known as 100 MPH tape is not only the second most important building material, it is also used to keep boats afloat, airplanes in the air and cars on the road, or anything else that needs to be held together, often permanently! Also used to repair holes in their clothing, shirts, jackets, jeans etc, in first aid as a band aid or splint and they say it will even kill a planter's wart.

Fast Food = A motorcyclist riding in bear country. That goes for mosquito territory too.

Frost Heaves = Broken up roadways caused from the expansion and contraction of the ground under the pavement, do to freezing and thawing, in other words rough, bumpy and sunken roads.

Gold Poke = the small usually leather bag that the miners kept their gold in.

Great Land = Great North, North Country, Far North and so many more are ways of addressing Alaska and Yukon.

Grizz = my friendly fury wilderness friend. Otherwise known as Brown Bear, Grizzly Bear, Kodiak Bear or scary bear, but I regress.

Hard Rock Mining = came into play when the miners doing placer mining went up stream as they looked for more loose gold until they found a vain in the solid rock. Then they started to tunnel through the solid rock and into the mountain following the gold rich quartz veins to retrieve the gold.

Highways = In Alaska and Yukon they call anything that you can drive on a Highway. I think it is their sense of humor coming out brought out from long dark winters. Many are not paved and just because you can drive on it doesn't mean that you won't get stuck in some hideously deep pot hole along the way.

Hooch = the liquid that sometimes forms on top of the sourdough starter. It is a form of alcohol and yep the miners drank it! They must have been desperate for booze, as it sure does not smell too good.

Hub and Spoke = the term I use to describe how we use the Kick. We try to find a central location to set up a base camp and take the Kick on day trips in the area. This way we save on fuel and do not waste time looking for a new campsite every night.

Ice Worm = Ice Worms are the real thing! Not just in the wild imagination of Robert Service's, "The Ballad of the Ice-worm Cocktail", similar to the earthworm, but just ½ inch long and thin as a thread. They thrive in icy temperatures that would seem impossible for most life. Little is known about their life style. They do not like the sun or heat, preferring to make their appearance at dusk. They have been seen standing upright, waving about in what is thought to be, an effort to catch food such as red algae and pollen, from a glaciers runoff.

Inukshuk = meaning a likeness of a person. These stone figures (as seen on the cover of this book) were used by the Inuit travelers, in the far north, to give direction and as a beacon to show the way for those who followed. It meant safe passage, where to find food, water and shelter along the way. You will see many modern day replicas along the roads today, wishing you safe travels.

Ish = if you see this strange word in my writings, it means "about" as in 2 hours, ish or about 2 hours. It is an often used word up north, there might be a moose in the road, don't you know or the fish are biting and you just have to stop, not to mention road construction, washouts and potholes.

Kick = the name we have given to the vehicle (rig) we tow behind our motorhome, Rika (other rig)

Lower 48 = because Alaska is separated from the other 48 states on the North American continent, it refers to those states as the Lower 48. Hawaii, of course, is not connected to North America so is not included in the state count.

Made in Alaska = this program is designed to promote products and handicrafts made or manufactured in Alaska. All Made in Alaska items are created by in-state producers using, to the greatest extent as possible, Alaskan resources and materials to complete the product. Be sure to check on the border crossing regulations if it is a big ticket item; ivory; fur etc.

Meals on Wheels = bicyclists traveling through mosquito and bear country. They are slower and easier to catch than Fast Food!

Midnight Sun = it really does stay up all night in the summer.

Moose Droppings = Also known as Tundra Pecans, Moose Nuggets or Moose Poop! Yes, you got it, no need to say more. Moose leave it everywhere!

Mosquitoes = often, mistakenly, referred to as the state bird, which of course is the Willow Ptarmigan.

Muskeg = boggy or swampy areas that little other than water loving plants and trees can grow. They are throughout the far north. If you drive your rig into one of these bogs it will sink out of site!

Northern Lights = see Aurora Borealis

Nugget = Well you may think I mean "gold" nuggets, but in this book a Nugget is a hint that might help you on your trip north.

Outside = when spoken by an Alaskan, this word means somewhere other than Alaska such as the lower 48, or anywhere else in the world, outside Alaska.

Penguin = a flightless bird, "**not**" found up north!

Permafrost = ground remaining frozen 2 years or longer if it is of the continuous, or discontinuous if not frozen continually. The bottom line is it covers the entire Arctic region and the alpine regions of mountains (even in the lower 48. Permafrost can be over 1500 feet deep.

Potholes = A hole in the road, big enough to lose your rig in, the rest are just bumps and divots.

Placer Mining = is typically panning or sluicing for loose gold nuggets or flakes in the gravel of stream beds. Placer mining typically comes before hard-rock mining.

Rig = the vehicle you will be taking be it car, bike, motorhome, trailer etc.

Rika= that's what we call our motorhome, after Rika's Roadhouse in Big Delta, AK. You get it don't you? Our motorhome is a "road house", house on the road. Rika's Roadhouse is a great stop for a Bear-claw!

Roadhouse = waypoints, situated along major transportation routes throughout the north, providing a comfortable place for early-day travelers, Rika's Roadhouse is one.

Scenic Byways = The National Scenic Byways Program was created to recognize outstanding roads that celebrate beautiful landscapes throughout the United States. Alaska has its own State Scenic Byways program as well.

Silver Hand = a program designed to identify authentic Alaska  Native handicrafts. The official symbol is the Silver Hand seal. The artisans using this symbol are also Made in Alaska certified. Check for what permits and paperwork you may need for border crossings if you buy any big ticket items.

Skookum = a word from Chinook Jargon, meaning strong, as in fast flowing river water. It has evolved to be used in describing a strong person or a good situation as well. Anything Skookum is good, fast, strong and the like.

Snow Mobile = also known as Snow Machine or Snow Go depending on where you live. They are the favored means of transportation in the winter (other than the dogsled) when one needs to get somewhere that the car won't go. They will never replace the dogsled completely, I am glad to say. There just isn't anything better than watching a team of dogs racing, pell-mell, across the snow, giving it their all! Without a doubt they love what they do.

Sourdough = goes back in history as far as 4000 years, to Egyptian times. The miners treasured their sourdough starter as much as the gold they sought. They tended to it carefully, even to tucking it into their shirts, next to their body, to keep it warm and healthy during the cold winters, that is why they are called "Sourdoughs" they started to smell just like their starter. If you have ever smelled sourdough, you will understand. As long as they had the starter and some flour they could survive. It is said that wars were fought over prized starters. Some treasured starters are pasted on from generation to generation. The famed San Francisco Sourdough Bread is said to be from starter originating in the gold rush days of early California. Sourdough starters each have their own distinct taste and "smell". Natural yeast organisms from the air act together, chemically with the dough to give it leavening action.

Tourist = someone who comes to *look "at"* instead of being a wanderer and adventurer of this Great Land. Given a chance it will, seep deep into your soul and forever draw you back. If this happens you will no longer be a tourist. Take time, to learn and *be a part* of this last frontier. It is worth the effort.

The Mountain = Denali, Mt. McKinley, Great One all these names are used when we talk about the tallest mountain in North America (20,320 feet). The Mountain because there is only one like it in the world, Denali was the Athabascan word for the mountain (meaning the high one) and McKinley, named for William McKinley of Ohio, who at in 1896 was a Republican candidate for president by the by, this was a ploy to get him to visit Alaska. It didn't work, as he never showed up. In 1975 Alaska officially renamed the mountain, Denali but the Federal Board of Geographic Names has not recognized this action.

Tow or Toad = is the vehicle (rig) towed behind a motorhome (other rig). We call ours the Kick.

Trading Post = in the past they were supply centers where one would get what you need to survive in the wilderness. Today you can find trinkets to buy and bring home. Remember to look for the *Made in* AK/YT and or *Made by* symbols if you are looking for authentic treasures.

Tundra = a treeless plain with moist soil on the surface and frozen subsoil.

Weather = don't ask what it's going to be just be prepared for what comes your way and dress in layers.

Wi-Fi = Many of the RV parks will keep you connected as well as coffee houses, libraries and some enterprising stores, where they are hoping to get your business as well.

Yukon = The Yukon – The Yukon Territory – Yukon Territory – YT, YK, they all seem to be used at one time or other. Old school it was always "The Yukon" but more recently "the" was dropped and Territory was added. I tried to get to the bottom of the issue by asking different individuals along the way. I think I got as many different answers as questions I asked. So you decide I still like The Yukon.

Wolf, Denali NP

Greater White Front Geese, Deadhorse

Caribou, Deadhorse

BIRD LIST

This is a list of some of the birds we saw this summer. I am not an expert in birding and this is not a complete list and I most likely have forgotten a few along the way. I enjoy trying to identify the birds I see and the ones that I can't identify, I enjoy anyway. I often hear folks say they did not see any wildlife while they were up north but as you can see by my bird list, one can, with little effort, see a great variety of our little feathered friends. I did not even add the birds I have seen in past trips. If I had, there would have been quite a few more on my list.

LOON - COMMON
GREBE - HORNED
CORMORANT - DOUBLE-
   CRESTED
SWAN - TUNDRA, TRUMPETER
GOOSE - GREATER WHITE-
   FRONT, SNOW, BRANT,
   CANADA
MALLARD
NORTHERN PINTAIL
NORTHERN SHOVELER
WIGEON - AMERICAN
CANVASBACK
RING - NECKED DUCK
SCAUP - GREATER
LONG - TAIL DUCK
SCOTER - SURF, WHITE-
   WINGED
GOLDENEYE - COMMON
MERGANSER - RED-BREASTED

HARRIER - NORTHERN
HAWK - SHARP-SHINNED,
   NORTHERN GOSHAWK, RED-
   TAILED, ROUGH-LEGGED
EAGLE - GOLDEN, BALD
OSPREY
FALCON - MERLIN, AMERICAN
   KESTREL, GYRFALCON,
   PEREGRINE
GROUSE - SPRUCE
PTARMIGAN - WILLOW, ROCK
CRANE - SANDHILL
PLOVER - SEMIPALMATED
KILLDEER
YELLOWLEGS - LESSER
SANDPIPER - SPOTTED,
   UPLAND, WESTERN
WHIMBREL
SNIPE - COMMON
PHALAROPE - RED-NECKED

JAEGER - LONG-TAIL, PARSITIC
GULLS - BONAPARTE'S, MEW,
 HERRING, GLAUCOUS
KITTIWAKE - BLACK-LEGGED
TERN - ARCTIC
DOVE - ROCK
OWLS - SHORT-EARED,
 SNOWY, GRAY
HUMMINGBIRD - RUFOUS
KINGFISHER - BELTED
WOODPECKER - DOWNY,
 PILEATED
FLICKER - NORTHERN
SHRIKE - NORTHERN
JAY - STELLER'S, GRAY
MAGPIE - BLACK-BILLED
RAVEN - COMMON
CROW - AMERICAN
LARK - HORNED
SWALLOW - BANK, VIOLET-
 GREEN, TREE, CLIFF, BARN
CHICKADEE - BLACK-CAPPED,
 BOREAL, CHESTNUT-BACKED
NUTHATCH - RED-BREASTED

DIPPER - AMERICAN
KINGLET - RUDY-CROWNED
WARBLER - ARCTIC,
 BLACKPOLL
BLUEBIRD - MOUNTAIN
THRUSH - VARIED
ROBIN - AMERICAN
STARLING - EUROPEAN
WAXWING - BOHEMIAN
NORTHERN WATERTHRUSH
SPARROW - AMERICAN TREE,
 SAVANNAH, GOLDEN-
 CROWNED, WHITE-
 CROWNED, FOX
JUNCO - DARK-EYED, SLATE-
 COLORED
LONGSPUR - LAPLAND
BUNTING - SNOW
BLACKBIRD - RED-WINGED,
 RUSTY
GROSBEAK - PINE
REDPOLL - COMMON
PINE SISKIN

ANIMAL LIST

ANIMALS	# SEEN	ANIMALS	# SEEN
BLACK BEAR	19	HOARY MARMOT	17
BROWN BEAR/Griz	21	MOOSE	51
POLAR BEAR	0	MUSK OX	ABOUT 40
BEAVER	7	PIKA	A FEW
BISON	9	PORCUPINE	3
CARIBOU	45	RIVER OTTER	6
CHIPMUNK	LOTS	SEA OTTER	5
COYOTE	3	DALL SHEEP	54 ISH
MULE DEER	23	STONE SHEEP	11
ELK	3	RED SQUIRREL	BUNCHES
RED FOX	12	ARCTIC SQUIRREL	SCADS
MOUNTAIN GOAT	11	VOLE	SOME
SNOWSHOE HARE	TONS	WOLF	8
LEMMING	6	WOLVERINE	1
LYNX	0		

You may be surprised by the numbers of animals we saw or more to the point did not see. Just because we were on the road for 92 days we should have seen a lot more, right? This is one of the myths I want to bust for you. Yes, there are a lot of animals out there, but it is a "Big" land too. I swear a 1,000 pound Moose can hide behind a 6 inch tree.

We did see countless numbers of "**Boulder Bears**" and "**Log Moose**" along the way. What? You have never heard of these animals? OK, to tell the truth that is what we call them when we thought we saw and animal and as we got closer it turned out to be a rock or tree instead. We are not the only ones with poor eyesight and a good imagination. While on tour with a group in Alaska, I was once asked what kind of big fish was making that "fin wake" in the river. I took a look and saw the water rushing past a stick. No matter how I tried to explain it, she was sure that it had to be something swimming by. The very rare **Denali River Shark** was created right then and lives on in the rivers of the north, not to mention the **Yukon Rock Dolphins** that frolic in the waters of the Yukon River. I fear that there may be someone out there that still believes in these mythical creatures.

To set the record straight, we did not see any **penguins** either, no matter how often I have been asked "will we see penguins on this trip?" I could not find any! Maybe it would be because they do not live this far north, you think? That is another one of those myths I feel compelled to bust. You may see those cute flightless birds in commercials, Christmas cards and in children's books, befriending a Polar Bear, but not in real life. They live way down south and never the twain shall meet, except at the zoo of course!

FOLLOW-UP

We have enjoyed sharing our adventures with you along in the Great Land up North. This has been a trip of a lifetime for us that we will not soon forget. We have experienced some of the best things and yet we have only scratched the surface and "yes" we will be back someday, soon.

Now to tie up a few loose ends, in case you were wondering:

[1.] After the shakedown run and me doing my share of driving to North Carolina and back, I did not drive Rika, not even once all summer long! We just did not do very many long days and Lorrin likes to drive. What can I say? For the record, I have driven Rika since our return home without a single scratch!

[2.] We only had a few problems with the rigs on our trip [a.] one broken hose clamp [b.] one small finishing nail in a tire for the Kick [c.] two small repairable chips in Rika's windshield [d.] we had to replace the awning after the microburst of wind destroyed it. [e.] one new starter motor for the Kick. All in all, we experienced very few problems!

[3.] The windshield cover that I made for the Kick protected it from getting chips. I will modify it to cover the hood as well, to keep the rocks out of the vents.

[4.] We did strike it rich in "Adventure" if not in gold.

[5.] My sourdough starter was a blast! We had many wonderful treats and I made all of our bread as well as lots of tasty deserts.

[6.] On the way home we did put up a sign in the Signpost Forest in Watson Lake, YT. It joins the more than 60,000 already there.

[7.] We did stay connected with the outside world every few days. [a.] Wi-Fi is available in most of the RV camps. [b.] Cell service is getting better, but there are still many areas that there is "0" service and some services do not work in the Yukon.

[8.] Even though many folks said it was a cold rainy summer, we felt that it was just fine. Yes, we had our share of rain, even snow. We only delayed travel or changed our plans once because of bad weather all summer long. We had no complains!

[9.] We saw our share of wildlife, caught our share of fish, we marveled at seeing "The Mountain", the flowers were beautiful and the leaves were just starting to turn as we headed south.

[10.] We departed before the nights got dark enough, to see any Northern Lights. We will just have to go back in the winter!

[11.] After returning home the 2 biggest problems for me, were getting use to the nights actually being dark *(I really like the long days of summer)* and I had to get use to people being everywhere. *(I really liked the solitude).*

[12.] No, I was not dinner for a griz.

[13.] No, we will never get rid of all the dust in the Kick.

[14.] And to answer the question, did we survive each other this summer? **"YES"** and to prove it, we were only home for 16 days before we were on the road again! This time we were only heading out for a month, first to Indianapolis to work Moto GP. We were Track Marshalls for this world class motorcycle race at the Brickyard. Next we headed southwest enjoying more National Parks and then finished up by working the last AMA Motorcycle race at Leguna Seca, CA but that is another story and another one of our adventures.

SOURCES

(A list of some of the sources that we used on the trip)

Alaska Almanac, Facts about Alaska
Alaska Fishing
Alaska Gazetteer
Alaska Official State Vacation Planner
Alaska's Wild Plants
Bells Alaska Highway Mapbook
Computer mapping program
Internet searches
Museums and sites of interest along the way
Petersons Field Guide to Mammals/Tracks
Sibley Guide Book to Birds
Simply Sourdough - The Alaska Way by Kathy Doogan
The Alaska Photographic Journal the Trail of '42
The Mile Post
TravelAlaska.com and related websites
Walking Tour pamphlets (free at visitor centers along the way)
Wildflowers along the Alaska Highway

Rika's Roadhouse, Big Delta State Historic Park,
Delta Junction

Lorrin dips one finger in the Arctic and I really did swim!

Our wish for you in all your travels:

That you miss the pot holes, washboards and frost heaves!
That the skies are always blue over your heads!
That you see those Grizzly Bears, before they see you!
And that you will get home,
One hour before the mosquitoes find you!
See you on the Alcan!

Grizzly sow and cub, Denali NP   Fisherman & Brown Bear,
                                       Wolverine Lake, AK

Moose Wrangell-St. Elias NP, AK   Spruce Grouse, Canol Rd, YT

Caribou, Top of the World Hwy near Boundary, AK

TO ORDER:

RAMBLING BY RV THROUGH ALASKA & YUKON TERRITORY

Available at: rvdrivesmart.com
or Mail: $16.95 Plus $2.00 shipping & handling to the address below.

Also available from Drive Smart Publications:

DRIVE YOUR MOTORHOME LIKE A PRO, by Lorrin Walsh
A complete guide to professional driving, techniques for beginners to experienced drivers.

At:
rvdrivesmart.com
or mail $12.95 to:
Drive Smart
PO Box 3690
Silverdale, WA 98383-3690

DRIVE YOUR MOTORHOME LIKE A PRO is also available on **DVD** by Lorrin Walsh and Mark Polk of RV Education 101. Mark is the author of "THE RV BOOK" and the Nation's leading producer of RV training videos. Mark is also known as the "RV Savvy Guy" on RVTV. The "DRIVE YOUR MOTORHOME LIKE A PRO" DVD can be ordered at rvdrivesmart.com or rveducation101.com

Order these RV publications for you & your traveling friends.

Nyla Walsh, a native of Washington State, grew up loving the out of doors and camping with her family in the Northwest. After marrying, her love for nature and travel continued and expanded across the United States via RV's. Nyla always dreamed of traveling to Alaska and finally got her chance in 1989. Her heart was forever lost to the allure of the far North.

She has worked on cruise ships in Alaska and around the World. As a tour director she guided guests throughout Alaska and Yukon, sharing with them this unique destination. As well she has traveled with her husband in their motorhome throughout this Great Land. Along the way she has gathered a treasure trove of stories and knowledge about where to go, what to do and how to prepare for travel and adventure in the remote lands of the Last Frontier.